IMAGES
of America

AROUND
BOULDER CITY

IMAGES
of America

AROUND
BOULDER CITY

Cheryl Ferrence for the Boulder City
Museum and Historical Association

ARCADIA
PUBLISHING

Published by Arcadia Publishing
Charleston SC, Chicago IL, Portsmouth NH, San Francisco CA

Library of Congress Catalog Card Number: 2008924305

For all general information contact Arcadia Publishing at:
Telephone 843-853-2070
Fax 843-853-0044
E-mail sales@arcadiapublishing.com
For customer service and orders:
Toll-Free 1-888-313-2665

Visit us on the Internet at www.arcadiapublishing.com

To the "Eighties Ladies":
Julia Kaighn, Lola Frazier, Marie Sullivan, and Nellie Softchin.

CONTENTS

ACKNOWLEDGMENTS

Thanks to photographers, for capturing moments in time; to collectors, for saving pieces of history; to donors, for giving to museums, libraries, and historical societies; and to archivists, for preserving the historic treasures.

Unless otherwise noted, the photographs in this collection came from the Boulder City Museum and Historical Association.

I would like to thank the following family and friends for their help: Jim Beneda, Nevada Raney Davis, Mary Duciome, Evelyn and Jim Harrington, Dorothy Helm, Pat Klinger, Marilyn and Richard Neidlinger, Mike Penuelas, Sid Raney, Gene Segerblom, Roger and Roseanne Shoaff, and Tony and Bobbie Werly.

I owe a special debt of gratitude to Karen Cowan of the U.S. Bureau of Reclamation, Lower Colorado Region.

Thanks to Patrick Baird, Lake Mead National Recreation Area; Kathleen War, University of Nevada–Las Vegas Special Collections; John E. Bromley, Union Pacific Railroad Museum; Bee Valvo, Cline Library, Northern Arizona University; and Greg Corbin, Nevada State Railroad Museum/Boulder City.

Thanks to Hannah Carney, my editor at Arcadia Publishing, for her enthusiasm, patience, and guidance.

I appreciate the encouragement I received from my family: Will, Kelley, Billy, and Jack Ferrence; Jim, Christy, Carmela, and Giacomo Ferrence; and my mother, Beulah Hopson.

Most of all, I would like to say thank you to my husband, Bill Ferrence, for making it possible for me to do "anything I want."

INTRODUCTION

"The eyes of the whole United States are on Boulder Dam, and hundreds of thousands of observers and sightseers will visit this project during the construction period alone. I don't think you of Las Vegas really realize the magnitude of this project from the tourist angle alone. I hardly think it can be underestimated!" This quote was made by Secretary of the Interior Ray Lyman Wilbur in an interview with Las Vegas mayor E. W. Cragin and a representative from the *Las Vegas Evening Review Journal* on July 3, 1931.

Secretary Wilbur went on to say, "We expect to create a national monument here, and to develop the tourist possibilities to the greatest degree. The land is already withdrawn, and just as soon as justified, we will start on this phase of the situation. Boulder Dam and the lake it creates will be one of the real wonders of the world, and in my opinion will be the premier attraction of all the national parks and monuments."

The secretary pointed out, "There will be a peculiar problem in connection with this lake which will make direct supervision by the government necessary at all times. The level of the lake will not be anywhere near constant. It will vary as much as forty feet from time to time, and it will be necessary to build the resorts around the lake so that this will not affect them materially. . . . We plan to stock the lake with fish and sincerely believe it will become one of the finest resorts, for seven months of the year, there is in the world." Furthermore, he said, 'We propose to build the highway from Grand Canyon to the head of Boulder Canyon, and this would never be done if the government did not take over the whole area. Creation of a national monument will interfere in no manner with whatever development might otherwise be carried on within this area."

Regarding hotel facilities at Boulder City, Secretary Wilbur stated that "if private capital did not undertake this project, the government would make sufficient concessions to insure construction of a modern hostelry there."

Secretary Wilbur was correct, although he could not have imagined what has happened. In February 1932, it was reported that the number of visitors to the Boulder City Reserve had reached an average of 750 persons per day. The number of visitors entering the reserve was steadily increasing as the work on the dam progressed and as Boulder City more completely took shape.

The National Park Service took over the management of the entire area except the dam and Boulder City. People began to realize that a vast recreational area was opening up with the reservoir created by the dam. The fishing, boating, and sightseeing opportunities were easily accessed by train, by airplane, and by automobile. Hundreds of thousands of people discovered that the sunny desert country is one of the best vacation spots in the West.

The National Park Service began development of the huge region. The Lake Mead National Recreation Area, known as LMNRA, comprises 1.5 million acres. There is plenty of room to play. Park planners knew there would be a never-ending stream of visitors to the dam itself; there would be a demand for recreation facilities. The park service planned well.

The Lake Mead National Recreation Area is administered from the Boulder City headquarters. The park activities are coordinated there. The Lake Mead National Recreation Area continues to provide camping and picnicking spots, lodging, and facilities for fishing, boating, and hiking. Providing educational activities and seeing to the safety of visitors are the responsibilities of the park rangers. The park now has eight marinas, eight campgrounds, and five RV campgrounds with hookups. It is estimated that 7–8 million people visit the park each year.

No other reclamation project had the publicity that Boulder Dam, now Hoover Dam, received. Boulder Dam continues to be a top tourist attraction in the Southwest. It was the first, the biggest, and it was built during the years of the Depression by men from around the United States. Boulder Dam was known throughout the nation before the first bucket of concrete was poured.

In 2008, the Bureau of Reclamation reports that one million people take a tour of the dam each year and millions more drive over it.

Just eight miles from Hoover Dam and Lake Mead, 28 miles from Las Vegas, and located on the road that connects the two, Boulder City attracts thousands of tourists each year. Boulder City businesses continue to serve those tourists. An elegant hotel was built in Boulder City, as well as auto courts, filling stations, cafés, and curio shops. Today the hotel remains, and there are motels, restaurants, service stations, and retail shops. The Boulder City Chamber of Commerce and the Boulder City Tourism Commission work on projects to encourage tourism.

In October, an art show is held. In 1963, the hospital auxiliary sponsored an art festival to benefit the hospital. Fifty local artists participated in the first show. Now hundreds of artists from throughout the United States participate. Art in the Park is considered a top art show and attracts more than 100,000 people each year. The 60th Annual Damboree will be held in 2008. Damboree is an old-fashioned Fourth of July celebration that begins with a parade in the morning and ends with fireworks at night. In 1956, a reunion of dam workers took place at the Boulder Dam Hotel. They named themselves the 31ers because they arrived on the Boulder Canyon Project in 1931. The 31ers annual reunion is still held every year, but it is now the children and grandchildren of the 31ers and other guests.

Today the magnificent dam, the lake, the river, the desert, and the unique town of Boulder City attract millions of tourists each year. This book chronicles the development of visitor services around Boulder City from the early 1930s until the mid-1960s.

One

CONSTRUCTION CAMP
TO MODEL TOWN

Boulder City began as a construction camp to house the workers of the Boulder Canyon Project. As families arrived with the workers, the Bureau of Reclamation realized that the town should be a well-planned but mainly temporary town. The 10th birthday of Boulder City brought the realization that Boulder City was destined to grow. In a decade, the town had grown from a sand hill covered by desert bushes to what was considered a "model city of the nation." The town was famous for its lawns, trees, air-cooled modern homes, and refined, well-educated residents. This 1935 view, the sentry station to the Boulder Canyon Project Federal Reservation, is a reminder of the town's beginnings. Today, with a population of over 15,000, Boulder City continues to grow at a controlled pace (mandated by the citizens in 1979). The Lake Mead National Recreation Area is headquartered in town. The Bureau of Reclamation still occupies the administration building as the Lower Colorado Regional office. (Courtesy of Bureau of Reclamation.)

The Silver Spike Ceremony was held September 17, 1930, to signal the beginning of the railroad to the town site. The ceremony was held at the new Boulder Junction, near Bracken Junction, and was attended by thousands. The railroad would bring the materials to build the town on the site that would be named Boulder City. (Original work the property of the University of Nevada–Las Vegas, Las Vegas, Nevada, with the permission of the Union Pacific Railroad Museum.)

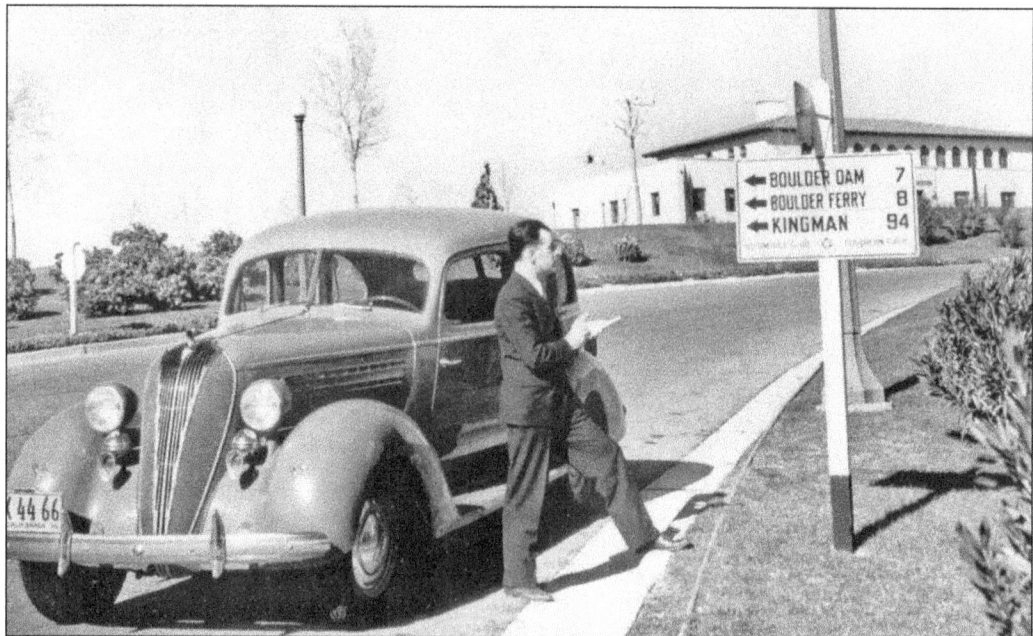

A California man, at the corner of Nevada Way and Park Street, is checking the Automobile Club of Southern California sign that shows the direction and distance from Boulder City to various locations. The Bureau of Reclamation administration building can be seen in the background. The bureau hired Saco DeBoer to plan the town. Part of his plan was to build the administration building on a hill with a park area leading up to the building. A portion of the park can be seen on the right.

In the fall of 1931, a sheet-iron shack was hastily built on Colorado Street, halfway between the construction of the water treatment plant and the truck route. It had a sheet-metal counter and apple boxes for seats. It was open for a few months when Jack Shields bought the restaurant. Shields was the brother of W. F. Shields, owner of Boulder City's first grocery.

The first grocery store and café in Boulder City was located at the bottom of Colorado Street on the truck route to the dam. From left to right, W. F. Shields, owner; Harry Buchanan, cook; and ? Shields are seen in this 1931 photograph. The family had owned a store some years before in Hesse's Camp on the Colorado River near the mouth of Las Vegas Wash. They later had another restaurant and cold drink stand on the government highway, below the reclamation camp. The Shields brothers were the first independents granted a permit to operate a restaurant on the reservation. (Original work the property of the University of Nevada–Las Vegas, Las Vegas, Nevada.)

11

Commercial development at the intersection of Nevada Way and Avenue B can be seen in this 1932 photograph. The building in the center was a drugstore, later owned by Robert Broadbent, that catered to both visitors and locals. In 1960, the federal government released control and Boulder City was incorporated. Broadbent, the first mayor of Boulder City, would go on to serve as Clark County commissioner and in the 1980s as the commissioner of the Bureau of Reclamation. (Courtesy of Bureau of Reclamation.)

The Southern Nevada terminal for the Union Pacific bus line was constructed by Frank Gotwals. The building housed a variety of businesses. The Boulder Café occupied the south end of the building. It was in the café that the chamber of commerce was formed in 1932. The terminal building, seen here on a snowy day, was at the corner of Arizona Street and Nevada Way. The building opened in 1932 and was demolished in 1941, after Gotwals declared bankruptcy. (Original work the property of the University of Nevada–Las Vegas, Las Vegas, Nevada.)

The 1942 grand opening of the Shell Station is shown from across Nevada Way. Arizona Street can be seen. The Uptown Hardware store is in the background on the right. The station was built on the corner of Nevada Way and Arizona Street, on the spot that had been the terminal building. Twenty years later, the station was completely torn down and a new Shell Station was built and operated by Bob Conners.

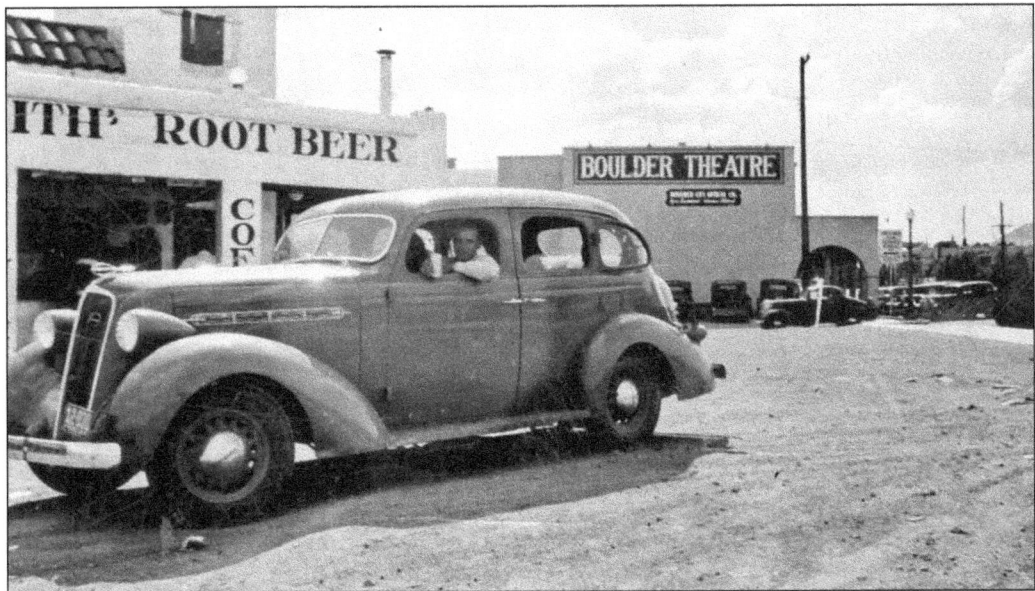

Smith's Root Beer Stand was a popular spot featuring carhop service. The Boulder Theatre can be seen in the background of this 1936 photograph. The man in the car is Frank Condon. Historian Virginia "Teddy" Fenton worked as a carhop. This image from the Teddy Fenton Collection was donated to the Boulder City Museum and Historical Association. Fenton was instrumental in forming the association and continued her support until her death in 2005.

To let everyone know that Boulder City had not folded up, Elton Garrett, shown here, published a one-page sheet called the "Boulder Dam Challenge." Garrett became the editor of the *Boulder City News* after serving as the first reporter for the *Boulder City Journal*, a section of the *Las Vegas Review Journal*.

A 1947 aerial view of Arizona Street, taken near the corner of Nevada Way, shows the business development in the 16 years of Boulder City. On the right, the Desertwear Shop had just moved into the new, modern building. The Boulder Dam Hotel is shown with the Uptown Hardware in the background. The Visitors Bureau is on the left across from the hardware store. The Nevada Rexall Drug located just beyond the Visitors Bureau provided vacation needs for travelers.

The new Desertwear Dress Shop and Nava-Hopi Trading Post opened in 1947. The shop located at 1327 Arizona Street, built for beauty, comfort, and convenience, was decorated with soft colors. Kay Hackwood is shown waiting on a customer. Leonard Atkinson was owner of both shops and managed the Trading Post, which featured Pinto Pottery (Desert Sands Pottery).

Fourth-generation potter Ferrell Evans, left, his father Arthur, and his sister Dorothy Thurston are shown making pottery. The Evans family developed a "local" industry. Earth was gathered from Utah, Death Valley, Valley of Fire, and other desert locations. Pinto Pottery was renamed Desert Sands Pottery. The business opened in 1946, and the last piece was produced in 1997.

Ida Browder's daughter Ida Browder (Kelley) can be seen can be seen on the running board of a car in front of her mother's restaurant. It was built in the "free enterprise section" of the business district. During construction, the family lived in a tent. The original boundary of the section started here, on Nevada Highway near Ash Street. Browder was one of the founders of the chamber of commerce.

Ida Browder, widow of an overseas soldier of World War I, had her own building constructed for the café. She arranged every feature for convenience and good taste. It was the first permanent business structure in Boulder City. This photograph was taken after a porch was added to the south of the original structure.

At left, Ida Browder (Mountford) is shown receiving the first quitclaim deed for commercial property. Shown from left to right are (seated) Bob Broadbent, mayor; (standing) Elton M. Garrett; Bob Glinski, Boulder City Chamber of Commerce president; and Curtis Blyth, Boulder City manager. Broadbent was the first mayor of Boulder City. As Boulder City's first businesswoman, Browder was given the honor as the first to buy her commercial lots. After the federal government left, the residents and business owners had the first right to purchase the property they had been leasing. The ceremony launched the beginning of the future expansion of the city, begun by this pioneer and continued by those who came after her. (Courtesy of Nevada State Museum–Las Vegas.)

One of the first permits the Bureau of Reclamation issued was to William Goodrich and Clarence Watson, who wanted to build a "tourist camp." The Boulder City Auto Court opened in 1931 with modern duplex units, single cabins, a filling station, and a grocery store (known as the "little store"). John Layton, one of the first employees, later opened Layton's Store on Utah Street.

O. L. Raney (left) and Don Belding can be seen in the window of the Boulder Laundry Company, under construction in 1948. Raney and Belding both arrived in Boulder City in 1931 and went to work for the Six Company Store, where they met. They became friends, then business partners. Raney and Belding became co-owners of a service station and the Boulder City Laundry. Both were exceedingly active in every civic enterprise that came along.

In June 1931, the Bureau of Reclamation received hundreds of applications for permits to open a business on leased land. This is a 1939 view of the theater and the recently completed Uptown Hardware Store and Apartments. The Boulder Dam Service Bureau opened in 1933 and was located upstairs in the theater building. (Courtesy of Bureau of Reclamation.)

When Visiting . . .
Boulder Dam

Be sure to stop at the SEVEN main points of interest as listed below:

1. **Nevada Lookout Point**
   Just before you reach the Dam.

2. **Top of Dam**
   Park on Dam and take elevator to powerhouse.

3. **Arizona Spillway Bridge**
   A few hundred feet from Arizona side.

4. **Arizona Lookout Point**
   Best view of upstream face and intakes.

5. **Observation Point**
   Near Babcock & Wilcox. Panorama of Lake Mead.

6. **Boat Landing**
   Excursions on Lake Mead:

To Dam	35 minutes	$ .75
Virgin Basin	3 hours	3.50
Grand Canyon	1 day	17.00
Grand Canyon	2 days	23.25

   Beach, free swimming, water sports.

7. **Boulder Dam Service Bureau**
   Located in Theatre Bldg., Boulder City, Nev. See the Official Boulder Dam Motion Pictures. Get your Free Windshield Sticker. Also Rest Rooms and Cold Drinking Water.

Free Motion Pictures	Writing Desks
Information	Loan Cameras
Souvenirs	Photographs
Postcards	Mail Box
Booklets	Stamps
Maps	Films

Boulder Dam Visitors Are Invited to See the

Official Government Motion Pictures

Showing the Building of

BOULDER DAM

From Beginning to Completion

Which Are Projected

Continuously

Free of Charge

in the

Boulder Dam Service Bureau

THEATRE BUILDING · BOULDER CITY

OPEN 7 A. M. TO 9 P. M.

Free Windshield Sticker

Earl Brothers opened the Boulder Dam Service Bureau under government permit on November 9, 1933. Brothers promoted the area to tourists. He worked with the government to produce a *Construction of Boulder Dam* film that was shown daily. As can be seen in this brochure, Brothers offered writing desks, loan cameras, film, a mailbox, and stamps, as well as souvenirs and maps.

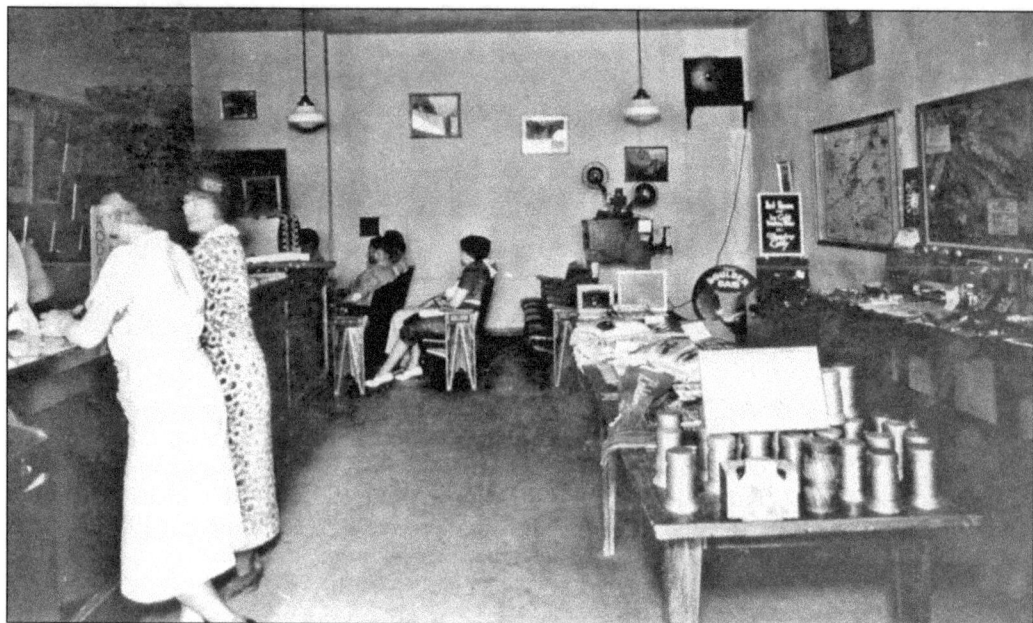

In the rear of the room at the Boulder Dam Service Bureau, a group can be seen watching the free movie of the Boulder Dam construction. Below is a close-up of the souvenirs and signs at the bureau. The Boulder Dam Service Bureau was located in the Boulder Theatre at this time, and the movie was run continuously throughout the day. (Both courtesy of Bureau of Reclamation.)

Earl Brothers, president and charter member of the Boulder City Rotary Club, is seen welcoming visiting Rotarians at a dinner. The Bureau of Reclamation administration building is pictured in the background. Brothers was interested in promoting the tourist industry in the area. As a friend of Frank T. Crowe, construction superintendent, he organized guided tours at the dam until the Bureau of Reclamation began the guide service. (Courtesy of Bureau of Reclamation.)

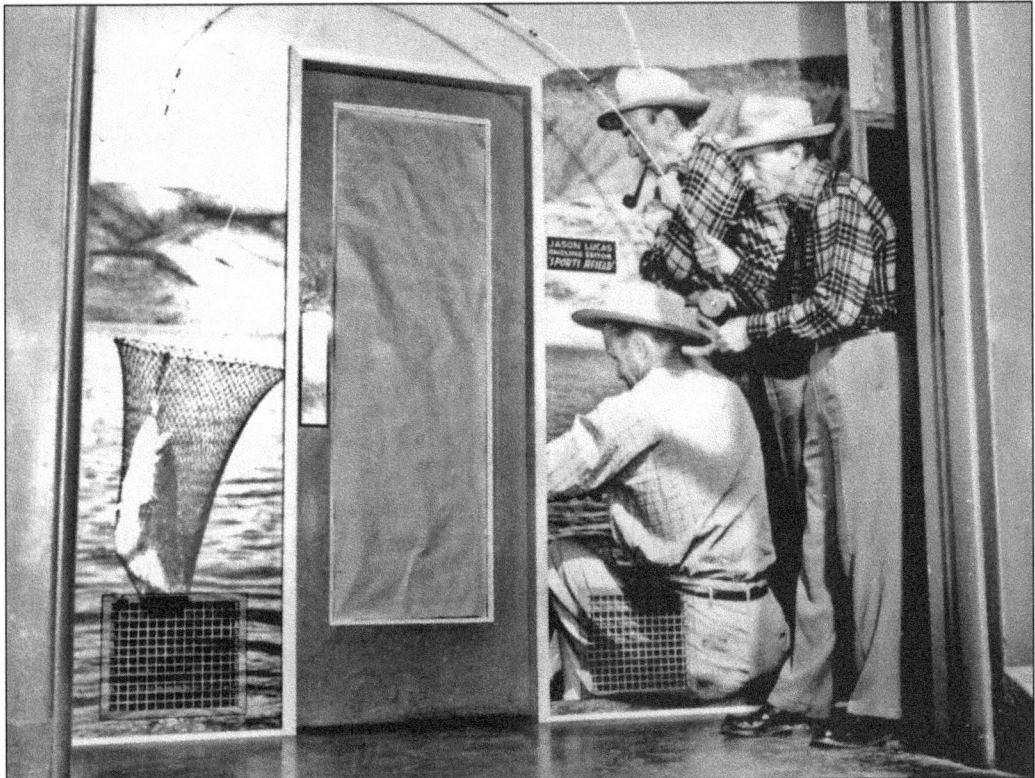

Jason Lucas is "beside himself" with a Visitors Bureau mural in 1948. Lucas was the angling editor of the popular magazine *Sports Afield* and the author of *Lucas on Bass Fishing*. His writings on bass fishing were legendary. (Courtesy of Cline Library, Northern Arizona University.)

A heavy rain transformed Arizona Street into a small river. From left to right, Buzz Belknap, Tick Segerblom, and an unidentified boy are shown taking advantage of the rain and practicing their river running skills. The Visitors Bureau can be seen across the street. The Belknap Photo Center is in the left background. The Visitors Bureau had moved across the street from the original location in the theater building. The bus terminal was located in the building at this time. (Courtesy of Cline Library, Northern Arizona University.)

Shown from left to right are Mark Swain, Bill Belknap, and Cliff Segerblom. This photograph was taken about the time the trio opened the Belknap Photo Center in 1950. The three talented photographers had been around the world but decided that Boulder City was the place to be. The shop was a stopping-off point for tourists and locals. Segerblom designed the unique building that is still in use today. (Courtesy of Gene Segerblom.)

The chuck wagon shown was Boulder City Chamber of Commerce's entry in the 1946 Helldorado Days parade. Mort Wagner, chairman of the Helldorado committee, announced that Art Klinger's black cow from Railroad Pass would follow the wagon, with young Roy Klinger following the cow on the family's white horse, Hirohito. The chamber of commerce was formed in 1932 and greatly influenced the Boulder City business community.

S. R. DeBoer, a prominent city planner, was hired to design the town. This 1934 aerial view of Boulder City shows the results of only three years' work. The seven main streets are named after the seven states drained by the Colorado River: Arizona, California, Colorado, Nevada, New Mexico, Utah, and Wyoming. The main street that runs through town is known as Boulder Highway, except in Boulder City, where it is Nevada Highway.

This aerial view of Boulder City shows the north side of the town just two years after the incorporation of Boulder City. The airport and the train depot can be seen. A new automobile dealership and other businesses are seen across the highway from the airport. (Courtesy of Bureau of Reclamation.)

Two

BOULDER DAM
OR HOOVER DAM?

The names Boulder Dam and Hoover Dam have both been used. When the Boulder Canyon Act was signed, the dam was planned for Boulder Canyon. As engineers surveyed the areas, the location was changed to Black Canyon. The dam became known as the Boulder Canyon Dam or Boulder Dam. The Bureau of Reclamation sometimes referred to the dam as Hoover Dam. In 1947, the dam was officially named Hoover Dam by an act of Congress. Whatever the name, sightseers began flocking to the edge of Black Canyon to view the construction activity, and except for the World War II years, the tourist activity has never ceased. More than 70 years later, "I've seen Hoover Dam, now I want to see Boulder Dam," is often heard. This is a view of Hoover Dam (Boulder Dam) overlooking the government cableway landing on the Nevada rim of Black Canyon. (Courtesy of Bureau of Reclamation.)

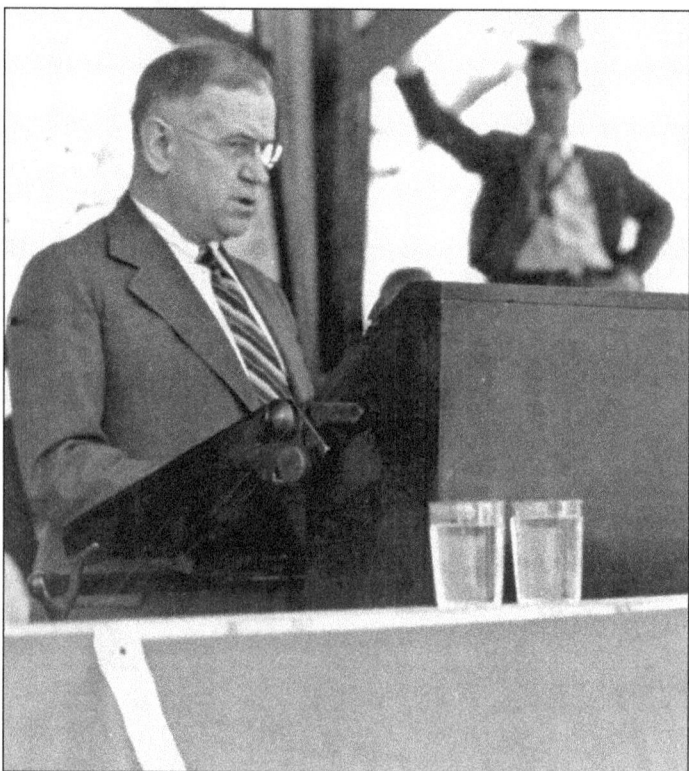

Above Secretary of the Interior Ray Lyman Wilbur is shown driving the silver spike to begin the Boulder Canyon Project. To the astonishment of many, he proclaimed that the dam would be named Hoover Dam in honor of President Hoover. Within weeks of Hoover's loss to Franklin D. Roosevelt, the new secretary of the interior, Harold Ickes, insisted that the dam had always been known as Boulder Dam. Ickes is pictured below delivering his address at the dedication. He referred to the structure as Boulder Dam. (Both courtesy of Bureau of Reclamation with permission of the Union Pacific Railroad Museum.)

Pres. Franklin D. Roosevelt, shown at the dedication, remarked, "Ten years ago this place where we are gathered was an unpeopled forbidding desert. In the bottom of a gloomy canyon, whose precipitous wall rose to a height of more than one thousand feet, flowed a turbulent, dangerous river. The mountains on either side were difficult of access, with neither road nor rail, and their rocks were protected by neither trees nor grass from the blazing heat of the sun. The site of Boulder City was a cactus covered waste. The transformation wrought here is a twentieth-century marvel." (Courtesy of Bureau of Reclamation.)

On the September 30, 1935, dedication day, the traffic through Boulder City was bumper to bumper. Every area of the dam was packed with spectators. A small part of the crowd of 20,000 who attended the dedication ceremonies at Boulder Dam can be seen in this image. Millions more would listen to the ceremony on radio. President Roosevelt said, "Gee, this is magnificent," as he saw the completed dam for the first time. (Courtesy of Bureau of Reclamation.)

In the January 15, 1929, issue of the *Las Vegas Age*, it was reported that "thousands of tourists continue to flock into Las Vegas. The road from town to the Boulder Dam site was a veritable caravan of motor cars early Sunday morning until long after dark." A portion of the incessant stream of tourists visiting the Boulder Canyon Project is shown around 1931.

In June 1931, the Bureau of Reclamation built a lookout point high on the Nevada side of Black Canyon's rim, downstream of the construction site. The observation point became known as the Crowe's Nest (for construction superintendent Frank T. Crowe). This unidentified family is shown on the Crowe's Nest in May 1932.

A construction worker (reminiscent of a high scaler) is shown working on the exhibit building on the Nevada side of dam. The building is located on the road to the Nevada spillway just upstream from the safety island. It housed a large room with a 30-foot model of the Colorado River Basin, a lobby, restrooms, and utility room. Seating capacity for about 90 persons was provided in the model room. A recorded lecture lasting about 15 minutes was synchronized with still pictures and presented on a screen. Below the exhibit building under construction shows the roof structure and one of the Nevada intake towers of Boulder Dam. (Both courtesy of Bureau of Reclamation.)

An announcement was made in 1939 that "hereafter the official guides of the Bureau of Reclamation will conduct parties to the Boulder Power Plant and other points of interest via the elevators in Boulder Dam." This view is of visitors purchasing tickets for the conducted tour. (Courtesy of Bureau of Reclamation.)

A Union Pacific Bus waits on top of the dam while passengers make the conducted tour to the power plant. From May 1 to October 1, the first tour of the day left the top of the dam at 7:00 a.m. and the last tour left at 10:15 p.m. The tours were 45 minutes long. (Courtesy of Bureau of Reclamation, with permission from the Union Pacific Railroad Museum.)

Pictured above, from left to right, is chief ranger Charles F. Peterson, ranger Lester Wedel, Roy Rogers, and ranger Bill Gettes during the filming of *Helldorado*. The picture was filmed at the dam in May 1946 and released on December 15, 1946. The picture starring Roy Rogers, Dale Evans, Gabby Hayes and Trigger; was set against the backdrop of Las Vegas and the annual Helldorado week. Below Republic Pictures is shown filming at the east gate at the lower portal road on the Nevada side of Black Canyon. (Both courtesy of Bureau of Reclamation.)

To the engineers, flood control, water storage, and power were the reasons for building the dam. While architect Gordon B. Kaufmann was in Boulder City to design the administration building, some changes were recommended. Kaufmann streamlined the engineering design by replacing the ornamentation with elements of modernism and art deco. This view looks down on the crest of Hoover Dam from the Nevada side. Photographer Cliff Segerblom posed his future wife, Gene Wines, in the foreground. Gene, a former teacher, was a freelance writer and collaborated with Cliff on many articles for national publications such as *Time*, *Life*, *Sports Illustrated*, *Arizona Highways*, and *Sunset* magazines. (Original work the property of the University of Nevada–Las Vegas, Las Vegas, Nevada.)

The visitors to the dam enjoy the work of art as well as the engineering wonder. This view shows details of design, including the bas-relief on the Arizona elevator tower. The cars and people on the dam were a daily sight. Hoover Dam was designated a National Historic Landmark and one of America's Seven Modern Civil Engineering Wonders. (Courtesy of Bureau of Reclamation.)

The Boulder Dam Amphitheater, located at the upstream end of the Arizona spillway, is shown filled to near capacity with 1,000 Rotarians and Rotary-Anns. As part of the Rotary International District Conference, an open-air luncheon was given on Boulder Dam, followed by inspection and tour of the dam and powerhouses. The April 15, 1940, event also included boat trips on Lake Mead and an open house at the Boulder Dam Hotel. (Courtesy of Bureau of Reclamation.)

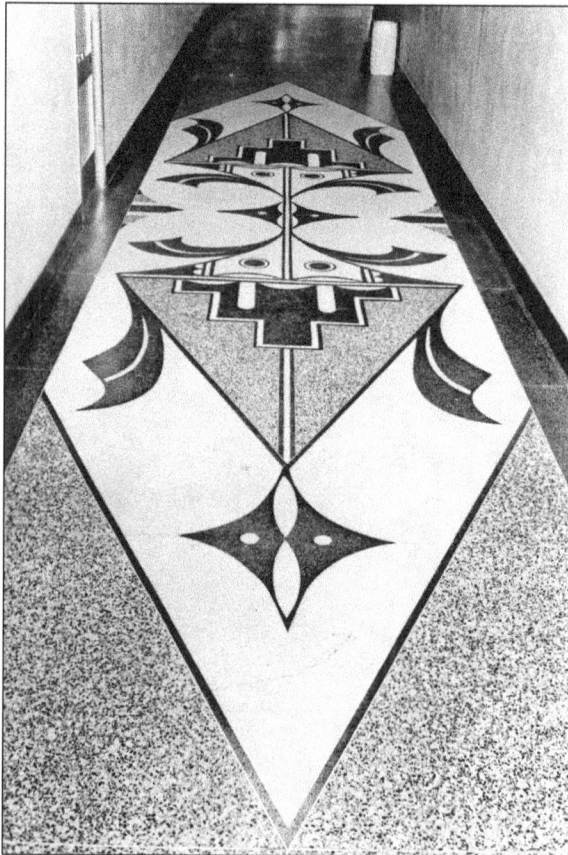

Denver artist Alan Tupper True assisted Kaufmann with decorations. Striking graphic Southwestern designs were incorporated in the terrazzo floors of the dam and powerhouse. True, who specialized in art depicting Western and Native American themes, found that their inherent boldness made them particularly adaptable for use in modern architecture. The floor design in the corridor of elevation 705.0 in the central section of the power plant is shown. It took almost a year to install the elaborate terrazzo. J. B. Martina Mosaics of Denver, Colorado, performed the work between 1936 and 1937. Italian craftsmen are shown pouring the under bed for the 3.5-inch terrazzo floor. (Both courtesy of Bureau of Reclamation.)

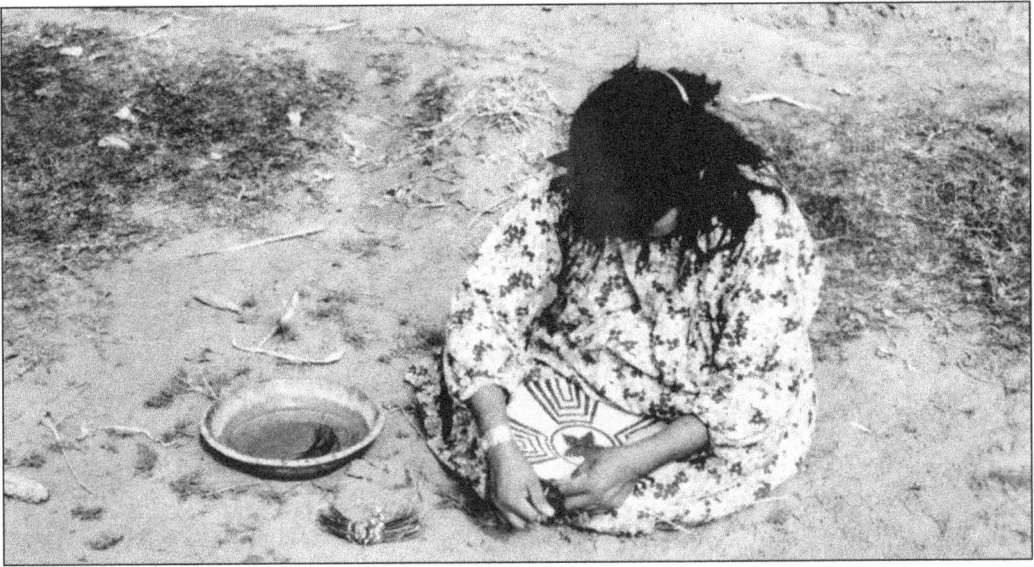

A Supai woman can be seen working on a basket. The Supais were noted for their beautiful basket making. The artist Alan True was also inspired by the colors the Native Americans used. The colors he chose were a deep, warm blue and black; a brown; concrete gray and a warm white; jade green bordering on turquoise; brilliant deep red; vermilion; orange; and canary yellow. All were tempered to harmonize with one another. (Courtesy of Bureau of Reclamation.)

Inspired by the Southwestern Native American patterns, artist Alan True used patterns that echo centrifugal themes, relating to the turbines in the power plant, as seen here. True also integrated the colors used in painting the turbine housings, overhead cranes, valves, and even doorknobs. (Courtesy of Bureau of Reclamation.)

A small ranger force was created. Reclamation employees were deputized as U.S. marshals. The rangers policed the dam and powerhouse. As seen in this 1940 photograph, the rangers patrolled Boulder Dam on small motor scooters. The found them very handy for the many stops and starts. (Courtesy of Bureau of Reclamation.)

Bureau of Reclamation guides began conducting official tours of the power plant and Boulder Dam in 1939. The guide force members are shown from left to right: Bill Dunn, Blackie Hardy, Bert Wadsworth, Pete Abbott, Don Scott, Philip Brinn, Paul Lytle, Bill Dalley, Lewis Pulsipher, and Buzz Brown.

Tyrone Power and his wife, Annabella, are shown visiting Boulder Dam on their honeymoon. Many celebrities and heads of state toured the dam, including the Crown Prince and Princess of Norway; the Crown Prince Frederich and the Crown Princess Ingrid of Denmark; and Prince and Princess Shrinagesh of Jahore, India. Many of them stayed at the Boulder Dam Hotel. (Courtesy of Bureau of Reclamation.)

The University of Nevada football team visits Boulder Dam and poses for a photograph in front of the Nevada elevator tower. The Wolf Pack arrived in Las Vegas on Thursday, September 29, 1938, to face the Arizona State College Lumberjacks (Flagstaff) on Saturday. It was the first meeting of the two squads and the first time playing in Nevada outside of Reno. On Friday, although the temperature was nearly 100, the squad visited the dam preceding a workout. (Courtesy of Bureau of Reclamation.)

Sculptor Oskar J. W. Hansen is shown checking the fabrication of the terrazzo star map at Boulder Dam. Hansen believed that future generations would look upon this monument and determine the exact date on which President Roosevelt dedicated the dam. (Courtesy of Bureau of Reclamation.)

On account of the many intricate patterns and metal objects placed in the terrazzo star map, it was necessary to invent a new terrazzo technique. Steel major pattern strips were set on legs into the base concrete. Steel piano wires were stretched to grade, and the patterns were laid from these. Workers are shown on Boulder Dam's Nevada safety island, where the terrazzo is located. (Courtesy of Bureau of Reclamation.)

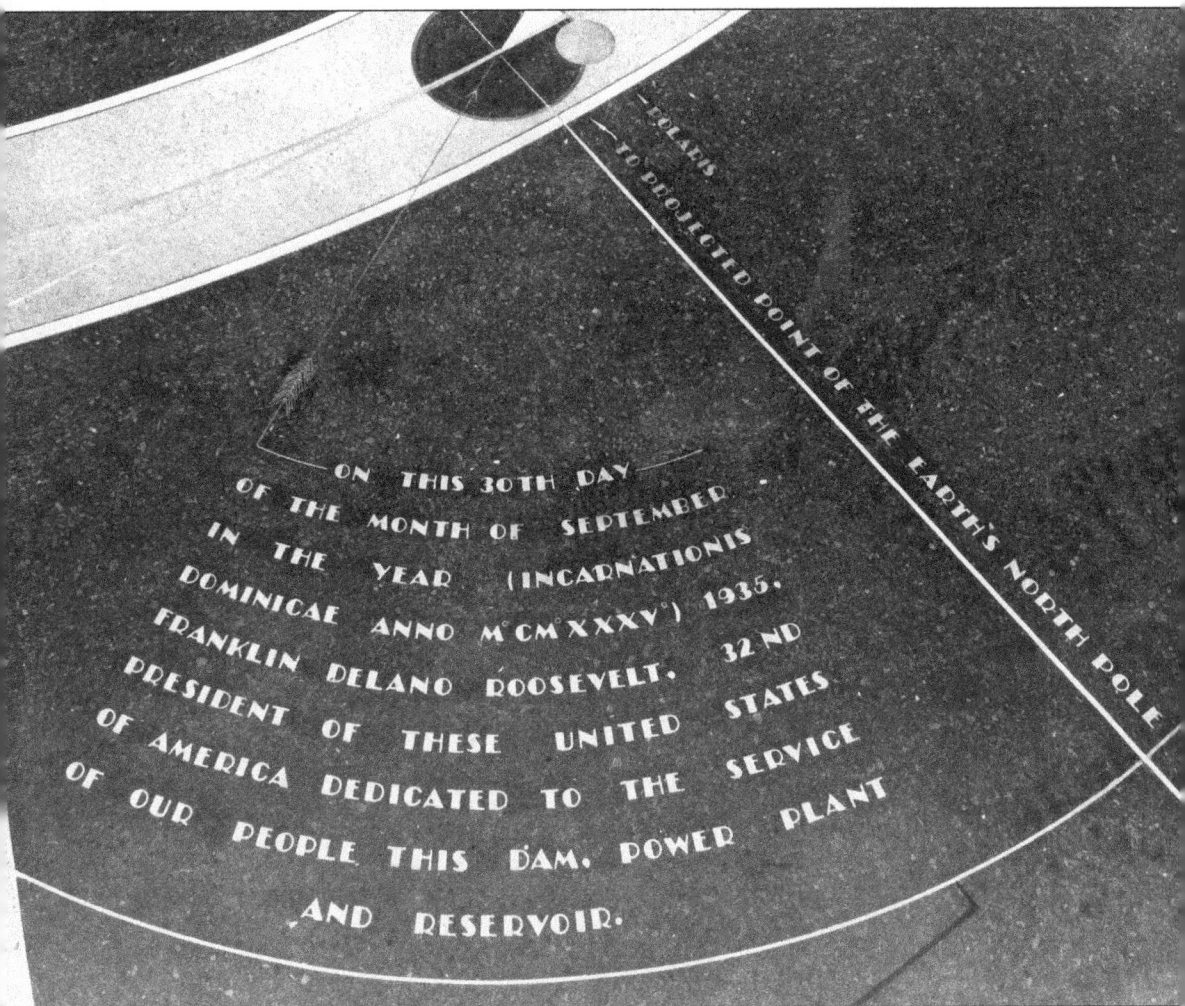

ON THIS 30TH DAY OF THE MONTH OF SEPTEMBER IN THE YEAR (INCARNATIONIS DOMINICAE ANNO MCMXXXV) 1935. FRANKLIN DELANO ROOSEVELT. 32ND PRESIDENT OF THESE UNITED STATES OF AMERICA DEDICATED TO THE SERVICE OF OUR PEOPLE THIS DAM. POWER PLANT AND RESERVOIR.

POLARIS

TO PROJECTED POINT OF THE EARTH'S NORTH POLE

This portion of the terrazzo star map shows the position in the equinox toward which the pole of the earth's equator pointed on September 30, 1935. Oskar Hansen was responsible for the greater part of the memorial art at Hoover Dam. His work includes the memorial plaque, the huge bronze winged figures, the bas-relief inscriptions on the elevator towers, the bald eagle floor design, and the compass and the zodiac. To Hansen, Hoover Dam represented the building genius of America. (Courtesy of Bureau of Reclamation.)

Illustrator Tony Mann was wed in a cableway skip while dangling over the project he pictured in the book *Hoover Dam*. The unique wedding of Mann and radio entertainer Hilma Parkhurst was held on December 18, 1931. Construction on the dam continued during the ceremony. Boulder City newsman Elton Garrett can be seen fourth from left in this photograph. A wedding dinner was held at Anderson Brothers Mess Hall.

The wedding of Minnie "Ma" Kennedy and Guy Edward "Whataman" Hudson was held in the Crowe's Nest on the Nevada side of Black Canyon on September 19, 1931. Ma Kennedy was the evangelist mother of Church of Four Square Gospel founder Aimee Semple McPherson.

In June 1933, boxer Max Baer defeated German Max Schmelling in front of 60,000 spectators at Yankee Stadium. That same year, Baer starred in the movie *The Prizefighter and the Lady*, playing the part of a bartender turned fighter. On June 14, 1934, Baer, left, knocked out Primo Canera to become heavyweight champion of the world. Baer is shown with Elmo L. Skuce on a skip line over the nearly completed dam. The workers were lowered over the rim of the canyon to go to work on the dam.

Discharge from the 84-foot needle valves was always a sight to see. This visitor, Gene Segerblom, is fortunate to have the great view shown in this Cliff Segerblom photograph. (Courtesy of Bureau of Reclamation.)

Dwight D. Eisenhower is shown here touring Hoover Dam in the summer of 1952. The retired general was elected the 34th president of the United States on November 4, 1952. (Courtesy of Bureau of Reclamation.)

Visitors to Boulder Dam are seen inspecting generator Unit N-1 in the Nevada wing of the powerhouse. The huge generators always attract attention. Artist Allen True chose vivid colors to contrast against the vast gray concrete area and specified red for the generator shells. True believed the use of color and decoration in industrial buildings was important. (Courtesy of Bureau of Reclamation.)

On April 4, 1941, visitors on a regular guided tour through Boulder Dam are entering the central section of the powerhouse. The guided tours were conducted daily and were 45 minutes long. (Courtesy of Bureau of Reclamation.)

Sculptor Oskar J. W. Hansen was appointed, after an open competition, to create memorial art. Here Hansen, wearing a suit with his hat in his hand, watches as one of the Winged Figures of the Republic is placed on the diorite base. In order for the blocks to be placed without marring, they were first centered on blocks of ice; the gradual melting permitted their being lowered into precise position. The bronze sculptures are 30 feet high and contain more than four tons of statuary bronze. The two winged figures flank a flagpole that is 142 feet high. Near the figures, elevated above the floor, is a compass framed by the signs of the zodiac. (Courtesy of Bureau of Reclamation.)

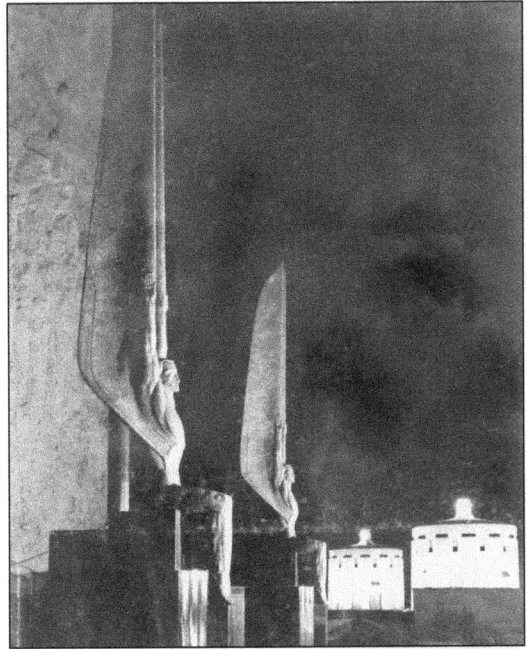

This night view of the bronze figures also shows the Nevada intake towers in background. Sculptor Oskar J. W. Hansen said, "Greater far than Hoover Dam is the object lesson it teaches in the humanities. Through tolerance, the unquenchable spirit of America will aspire, like the Winged Figures of the Republic on Hoover Dam, ever upward to keep our flag in the blue." (Courtesy of Bureau of Reclamation.)

A 1940s scene is of visitors to Boulder Dam showing great interest in the star map design on the floor of the safety island at the Nevada approach to the dam. The Winged Figures of the Republic and the flagpole can be seen. (Courtesy of Bureau of Reclamation.)

An early assignment of Bureau of Reclamation photographer Cliff Segerblom was to photograph work on the nearly completed Boulder Dam. He took this photograph looking downstream from the crest of Boulder Dam on September 28, 1940. It shows radio, newspaper, and newsreel men being lowered by the government cableway, on a skip, for a close-up view of the water flowing from the canyon wall needle valves. This image has been on exhibit at the Museum of Modern Art in New York City. Segerblom went to work for the Bureau of Reclamation despite the fact that he had never taken a picture in his life. Segerblom was also an artist. In 1969, he was commissioned by the navy to record the Apollo 12 splashdown in the South Pacific. The six watercolors he did as a result are displayed in the National Aeronautics and Space Museum. (Courtesy of Gene Segerblom.)

The new facilities, including the visitor center, parking structure, and a new penstock viewing platform, were opened to the public on June 21, 1995. The new facility was necessary to accommodate the one million visitors to Hoover Dam each year. (Photograph by Andrew Pernick; courtesy of Bureau of Reclamation.)

Three

TRAVEL BY AIR, RAIL, AND ROAD

Because the site selected for the dam was in a remote area, roads and rails had to be completed to build Boulder City and the dam. The road between the Boulder City town site and Las Vegas consisted of two tracks through the desert. In other areas, there were no roads or railroads. In 1932, the roads and rail were complete. Soon an airport was built. This is a view of the April 13, 1938, inauguration of Transcontinental and Western Airways (TWA) service in Boulder City. The airplanes, automobiles, highway, and railroad tracks in the background typify the seven years of progress.

The Ford tri-motor airplane used by the Grand Canyon Airlines in Boulder City–South Rim service is shown on July 29, 1936, at the field in Boulder City with the waiting room at left. Below is a photograph taken from the airplane. Boulder City is seen as the tri-motor circles the field and heads for the Grand Canyon. (Both courtesy of Bureau of Reclamation.)

The neatly laid out town of Boulder City is seen from 2,000 feet with Lake Mead in the background. The Grand Canyon capped with clouds is the view from the Ford tri-motor. This view is an hour's flight from Boulder City. (Both courtesy of Bureau of Reclamation.)

In 1931, Noel Bullock leased land from the Bureau of Reclamation to establish an airfield. On November 19, 1933, Boulder City's airport, Bullock Field, opened. Later the airport property came under the jurisdiction of the National Park Service. Glover Ruckstell obtained a 20-year concession contract with the park service. A mainliner can be seen from the arcade of the new passenger depot in 1938.

Glover Ruckstell signed an agreement between his company, Grand Canyon–Boulder Dam Tours (GCBDT), and Transcontinental and Western Airways (TWA). The agreement was that GCBDT would improve the Boulder City airport if TWA would lease it. This view of the recently completed airport service station and depot for the Boulder City airport is dated December 22, 1938. (Courtesy of Bureau of Reclamation.)

An agreement between Glover Ruckstell and TWA made it possible for this TWA mainliner to pick up passengers from the depot, as shown in the above photograph. TWA remained at the Boulder City airport until 1949. Part of those improvements included a new terminal. The terminal shown was built in the Pueblo style. The waiting room featured a wood-burning fireplace and an open, beamed ceiling. It included restrooms, a radio room, ticket office, and a manager's office. In 1958, the Boulder City Elks Club bought the building for use as a clubhouse. The Elks have made changes to the structure, but it is still in use today. (Both courtesy of Bureau of Reclamation.)

Several Boulder City boys are seen inspecting the navy airplanes. The midshipmen pilots and mechanics stopped in Boulder City and took some time to tour Boulder Dam on October 23, 1940. The pilots and mechanics returned to the carrier *Saratoga*, based in San Diego, California, to complete flight training. (Courtesy of Bureau of Reclamation.)

The hangar seen from the highway offers scenic flights. The building was once the hangar for Grand Canyon Airlines and TWA. The navy hangar can be seen in the background.

This 1962 aerial view of Boulder City shows the highway that connects Boulder City with Las Vegas. The airport is seen on the left, and the independent businesses on the right. The El Dorado Valley dry lake (playa) can be seen in the background on the left. (Courtesy of Bureau of Reclamation.)

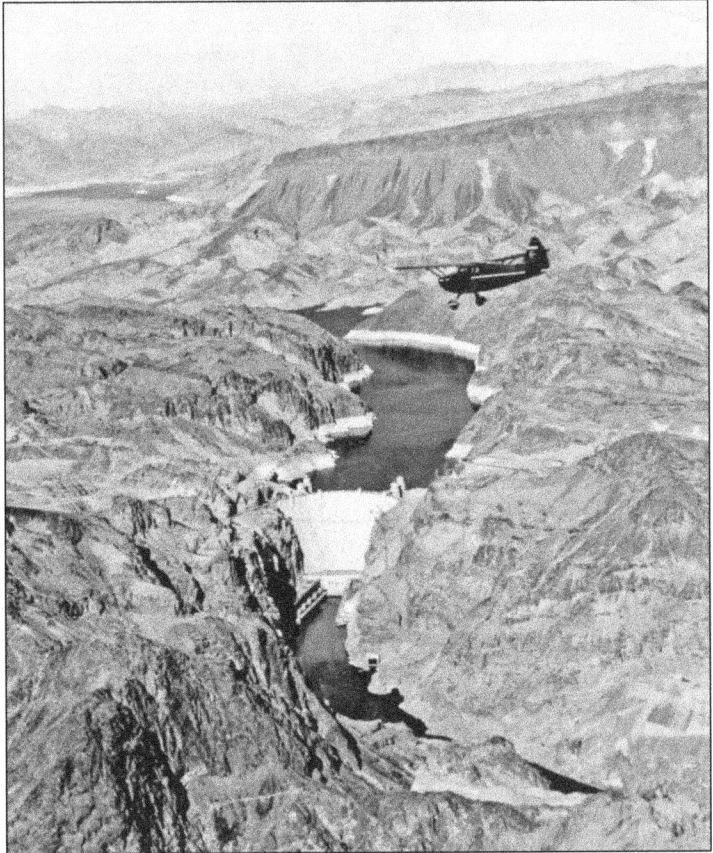

This spectacular view of Hoover/Boulder Dam and the surrounding area is that seen by passengers of the scenic flights over the dam and Grand Canyon. (Courtesy of Bureau of Reclamation.)

The Union Pacific Railroad built a 23-mile-long line extending from a point near Las Vegas on its Salt Lake–Los Angeles system to a site where Boulder City would be built. This photograph was taken on the day the silver spike ceremony took place. (Courtesy of Bureau of Reclamation, with permission from the Union Pacific Railroad Museum.)

The men shown working on the railroad are laying out the tracks for the Union Pacific Railroad branch line into the Boulder City town site. (Courtesy of Bureau of Reclamation, with permission from the Union Pacific Railroad Museum.)

The Union Pacific built sidings to the locations chosen for warehouses and other structures that would require direct train. Union Pacific crews are shown laying track in interchange yard in the Boulder City on February 2, 1931. (Courtesy of Bureau of Reclamation, with permission from the Union Pacific Railroad Museum.)

The Lewis Construction Company was awarded the contract to build the government railroad from Boulder City to the dam site. The railroad was completed in September 1931. Subcontractors Shanahan Brothers Construction Company are shown laying rails on the Six Companies construction railroad through Hemenway Valley. (Courtesy of Bureau of Reclamation.)

Conductor C. G. Duff is shown punching the first ticket on the Boulder City line for passenger Jo Watson on April 26, 1931. Construction of the Boulder City branch line of the Union Pacific Railroad was begun on September 17, 1930. Also seen is W. R. Armstrong, general manager, Los Angeles–Salt Lake Railroad (left) and train master N. E. McKinnon. (Original work the property of the University of Nevada–Las Vegas, Las Vegas, Nevada, with permission from the Union Pacific Railroad Museum.)

Four special trains brought nearly 2,000 Shriners to Boulder City, with delegations from Los Angeles, San Francisco, San Diego, Sacramento, Phoenix, and Salt Lake City. Boulder City chairman Bob Ferguson arranged for residents of Boulder City to transport the Shriners to the dam for the ceremonial services. The trains are shown in the Boulder City switchyard on April 17, 1940. (Courtesy of Bureau of Reclamation, with permission from the Union Pacific Railroad Museum.)

Ice can be seen on the water feeder in this John Westen photograph, taken at the Union Pacific Railroad yard in Boulder City. The Boulder City depot can be seen in the left background of this 1948 photograph. The train station opened on February 1, 1931. Two round-trip runs between Las Vegas and Boulder City were made each day. After the Union Pacific discontinued service to Boulder City, the depot stood abandoned. In 1974, the depot was sold to the Clark County Heritage Museum and moved to the museum complex in Henderson. It can be seen there today. The Nevada State Railroad Museum/Boulder City is located up the tracks from the area shown. From February through December, the railroad museum offers excursion train rides on Saturday and Sunday. Volunteers are aboard to explain the sights and tell the history of the railroad in this area.

The Boulder City train yard is shown. Union Pacific was responsible for building a 400-car switching yard in Boulder City. The government placed a contract for the construction of tracks from Boulder City to the Nevada rim of Black Canyon directly above the dam site. After completion, it was turned over to Six Companies for operation. At a point 6.25 miles from Boulder City, the government contractors started work on the remainder of the system. (Used with permission from the Union Pacific Railroad Museum.)

The canyon railroad built by Six Companies, Inc., winds along the Colorado River into Black Canyon. This steam locomotive is hauling muck from the dump hopper at the low-level mixing plant. It is traveling along the right-of-way above the river camp, which can be seen in the background, on January 28, 1932. (Courtesy of Bureau of Reclamation with permission from the Union Pacific Railroad Museum.)

Cecil B. DeMille's promotional tour of the Union Pacific train was to advertise the release of the Paramount film *Union Pacific*. These images show the train in Boulder City, Nevada. "Old 58" continued the Los Angeles–to–Omaha tour of the country. The run also coincided with the opening of the new Los Angeles Union Station. The film had been playing at the Boulder City Theatre and created much interest in seeing the special train. The woman in the foreground below is Gene Segerblom. (Both courtesy of Bureau of Reclamation with permission from the Union Pacific Railroad Museum.)

A large crowd attended the display of the nation's first streamliner, the "Train of Tomorrow." The *City of Salina* attracted the large crowd to see the Union Pacific Railroad streamliner on display at Railroad Avenue and Birch Street. This view of the crowd also shows the water filtration plant. (Used with permission from the Union Pacific Railroad Museum.)

The "Train of Tomorrow" is shown at Boulder Dam on March 9, 1934. The streamliner's opulent furnishings, impeccable service, and total comfort combined to lure customers back to the rail. (Used with permission from the Union Pacific Railroad Museum.)

In the 1930s, Union Pacific railroad introduced a lightweight streamliner passenger train. These trains set a new standard for luxurious train travel. Known as the "Train of Tomorrow," the nation's first streamliner, *City of Salina*, is shown in this dramatic image at the upstream face of Boulder Dam. Air-conditioning, reduced noise, and a better ride distinguished these trains from the steam-powered trains. Over the next seven years, nine more streamliners were added to the fleet. (Original work the property of the University of Nevada–Las Vegas, Las Vegas, Nevada, with permission from the Union Pacific Railroad Museum.)

Six Companies, Inc., was responsible for aligning and oiling six miles of road down the Hemenway wash toward the upper portals. Early in 1931, the 8-mile oiled surface was built between the town site and the dam site. The Black Canyon Highway was completed in the fall of 1931. Workers are shown mixing the oil finish for Hemenway Wash Road. (Both courtesy of Bureau of Reclamation.)

A road map does not show the difficulties met in building the roads and railroads. The rocky, steep surfaces and the great differences in the elevation of the points that had to be connected were a challenge. This view looks southeast at the equipment of R. G. LeTourneau and gives a glimpse of the challenge. LeTourneau was the subcontractor who built the U.S. Construction Highway. (Courtesy of Bureau of Reclamation.)

This 1932 view looks north at the Nevada road. Once the dam had reached its complete height, this road was connected to the roadway on the dam. An Arizona road was built to connect the dam roadway, making travel from Nevada to Arizona possible.

65

A typical way to travel in the early 1930s is depicted in this photograph of the Buck family. The Boulder City family is shown on an outing in the Southern Nevada desert around 1934. Eileen Buck (Conners) is shown standing behind the automobile.

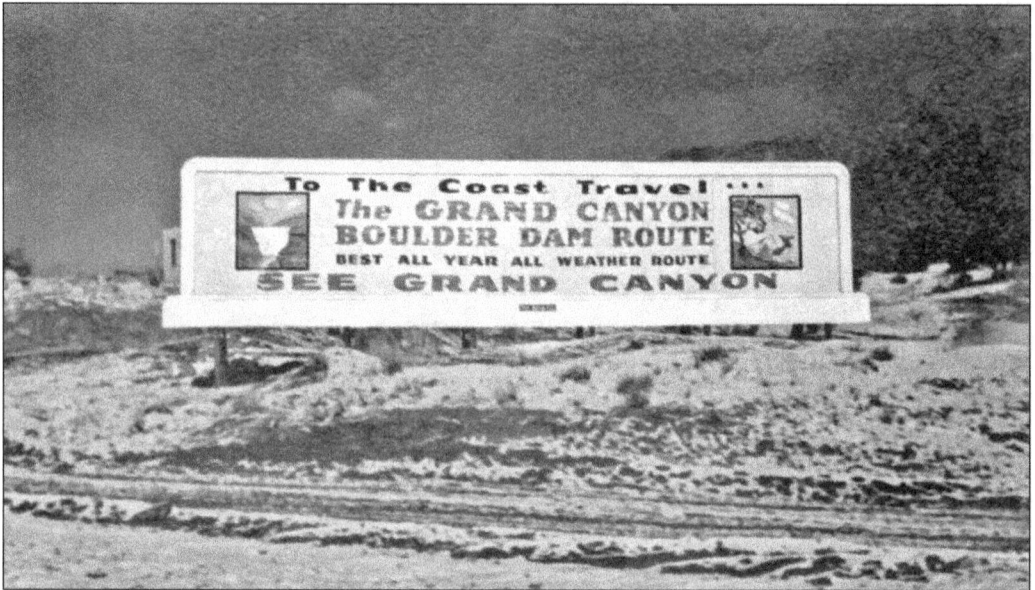

The Grand Canyon Route signs were placed along the highway; the one pictured here was in New Mexico.

Woody Williams (right), assistant construction superintendent, was the first to drive an automobile across the dam. On March 23, 1935, Williams took his Ford V-8 from Nevada to Arizona and back again. He wasn't deterred by the fact that three sections remained to be poured. He overcame the obstacles by putting down planks. Ted Davis (left) and ? Williams (center) accompanied him on the special trip. (Courtesy of Bureau of Reclamation.)

This was the scene two years after the first automobile crossed the dam. Private automobiles are parked on the dam. Union Pacific buses made two complete trips to the dam each day, one in the morning and one in the afternoon. (Courtesy of Bureau of Reclamation.)

This scene shows several people filling the radiators of their automobiles. The water tank was located at the bottom of the Hemenway Wash road. It was a convenience for those traveling in the hot, dry desert. (Courtesy of Cline Library, Northern Arizona University.)

The Union Pacific Railroad offered side trips on their Overland Route. Once the passengers reached Las Vegas, they could take an interesting 29-mile bus trip to see Boulder Dam and Lake Mead. One of the tour buses and a private automobile can be seen here. The side trip could be made between trains for as little as $4.65. (Courtesy of Bureau of Reclamation.)

This is an October 21, 1939, view of the recently completed highway to the new bathing beach located in Hemenway Wash on Lake Mead. The following advertisement was placed in the November 1, 1939, issue of the *Boulder City Reminder*: "We are glad to compliment the National Park Service on the completion of their new road to the Beach—Another Big Step Forward—Boulder City Chamber of Commerce." (Courtesy of Bureau of Reclamation.)

On December 7, 1941, after Pearl Harbor was bombed, director of power E. A. Moritz telegraphed Bureau of Reclamation commissioner John Page that "effective 5 p.m. the power plant has been closed to visitors. All persons and cars will be checked at boundary gates . . . and cars convoyed across the dam." The driver in this photograph, taken November 26, 1941, was not subject to the restrictions imposed less than two weeks later. (Courtesy of Bureau of Reclamation.)

The annual Gilmore Oil Economy Run began in 1936. Automobiles built by various American manufacturers were entered. Each year, the run began at Gilmore Stadium in Los Angeles. A 1941 entry can be seen traveling over Boulder Dam en route to Grand Canyon, Arizona. The winner of the 1941 Gilmore—Grand Canyon Run was a Studebaker that averaged 22.57 miles per hour. (Courtesy of Bureau of Reclamation.)

In this view of Boulder Dam, taken from the Nevada rim of Black Canyon in 1939, the highway to Kingman, Arizona, can be seen in the distance. The Arizona Highway Department began paving the dirt road between Kingman, Arizona, and the Boulder Dam Ferry on December 3, 1933. The road opened in 1935. (Courtesy of Bureau of Reclamation.)

Four

RIO COLORADO

The Colorado River was originally named Rio Colorado or "Red River" by the Spanish. The Colorado was unpredictable and at times would rise 50 feet overnight. The river was difficult to navigate because of the rocky terrain and the raging rapids. It was too muddy for fishing, and the currents were too fast for boating. Running the river wasn't a popular diversion; only a few hardy men had made the trip. For many years, man had dreamed of taming the mighty Colorado. The dream came true with the building of Hoover Dam. This photograph of the meandering river was taken from Monument Pass on June 27, 1929. Lake Mead began forming on February 1, 1935, when the gates of the diversion tunnels were closed. It is unlikely that this view will ever be seen again. (Courtesy of Bureau of Reclamation.)

The Boulder Canyon Project Board of Engineers is shown at the lookout point above the dam site on June 23, 1929. Pictured left to right are A. J. Wiley and Louis C. Hill, consulting engineers; John L. Savage, chief designing engineer; L. H. McClellan, electrical engineer; B. W. Steele, designing engineer; and Walker R. Young, construction engineer.

Ten years before construction of the dam began, barges with diamond drill rigs tested the rock beneath the river at Boulder Canyon and Black Canyon. Investigations went on for several years before Black Canyon was chosen. The ever-changing river made the drilling activities dangerous at times. Shown here are 36-by-15-foot diamond drilling barges at Black Canyon around 1922. (Courtesy of Bureau of Reclamation.)

In 1930, a Ford tri-motor airplane flies over the Colorado River in Black Canyon, near the future site of Boulder Dam. Scenic Airways was started in 1927 and became Grand Canyon Airlines. The company flew the new Ford tri-motor airplanes from Phoenix to the Grand Canyon. (Courtesy of Bureau of Reclamation.)

The boat in the front of the Colorado River excursion is the *Boulder*, followed by the *Miss Vegas*. The third boat is unidentified but operated by Murl Emery. The *Miss Vegas* was designed by P. L. Lacey, who launched the boat with great fanfare. *Miss Vegas* was in use for a short time. Lacey sold the elegant *Miss Vegas* to the Six Companies. Her paint was stripped and her railings and benches removed. She hauled dam workers and equipment through Black Canyon. She was scrapped at the end of the job, with her name carefully preserved on the bow.

The image above shows conditions at Williamsville, Nevada (also known as Ragtown), at the entrance to Black Canyon, near Cape Horn. The Boulder Dam Pier and Murl Emery's store were built and Ragtown developed here. The Boulder Dam Pier was built by P. L. Lacey, but the pier was in the way of dam construction and had to be removed at a loss of Lacey's entire investment. Murl Emery's boat service is shown. In January 1939, Emery estimated, "Sunday's visitors to the dam would run into more than a thousand cars." (Both courtesy of Bureau of Reclamation.)

Murl Emery's family ran the ferry service between Arizona and Nevada in the 1920s. He often ferried engineers and workers of the Boulder Canyon Project. A ferry is shown here around 1930. (Courtesy of Bureau of Reclamation.)

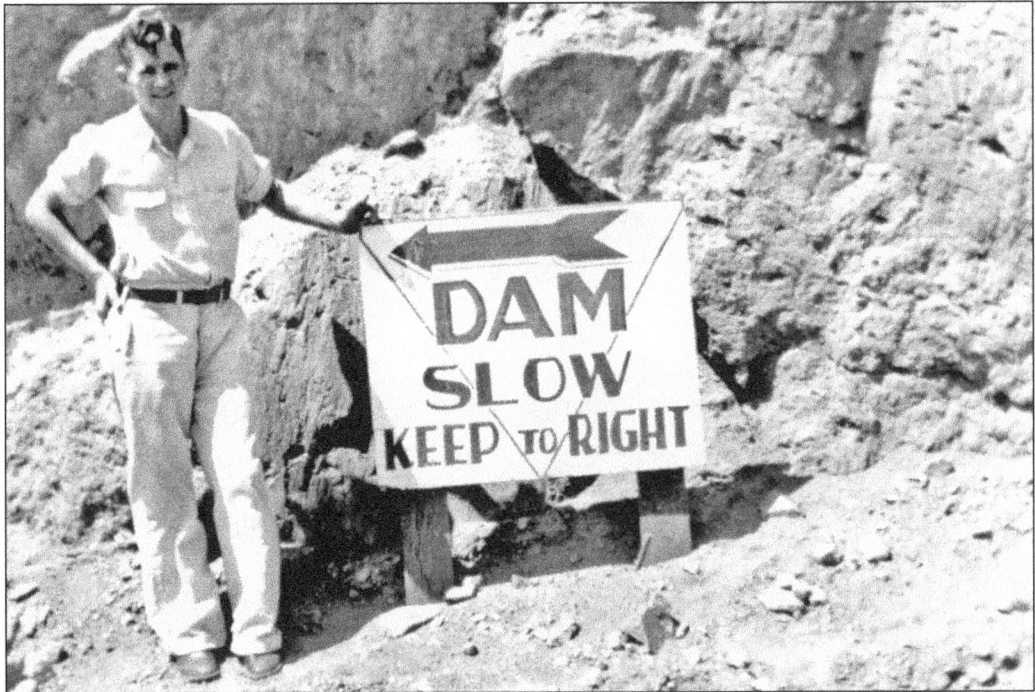

Boulder City had two companies of the Civilian Conservation Corps (CCC), referred to as Twin Camps. The boys were to build a highway around the rim of Lake Mead, make improvements to the airport, and develop tourist facilities in the Boulder Dam Recreational Area. One crew was sent to a remote area to put guardrails along the roads. This unidentified man near a construction sign was photographed in the 1930s.

Buzz Holmstrom is seen as he appeared when he arrived at the Boulder City boat landing after traveling alone in a rowboat the entire length of the Grand Canyon and Lake Mead from Green River, Wyoming. As he pulled into the boat dock at Hemenway Wash, he became the first person to navigate the river alone. (Courtesy of National Park Service.)

Buzz Holmstrom, in a boat he designed and built, navigated the entire length of the Colorado River across Boulder Lake (Lake Mead) to Boulder Dam (Hoover Dam). He is shown near the boat landing at Hemenway Wash on Thanksgiving Day, November 25, 1937.

Haldane "Buzz" Holmstrom was a 28-year-old service station operator from Coquille, Oregon. Holmstrom launched his boat on October 4, 1937, and when he reached Boulder City, he had covered 1,100 miles. He called it "a grand vacation." The entire trip was made by drifting with the current, but once in the still waters of the lake, he was forced to use the oars. He was offered a tow by one of Grand Canyon Navigation Company's boats, but he refused, preferring to finish the trip by his own power. It took him four and a half days to row the 112 miles. This shows Buzz touching the dam with a deliberate "thump." The young man was the guest of Jim Webb at the Boulder Dam Hotel. Buzz eventually returned to Boulder City and went to work for Grand Canyon–Boulder Dam Tours as a lead captain. He was expected to dress in a captain's uniform, greet the guests, and tell stories of his exploits. He didn't work there long; he was a shy, independent man, and the job didn't fit his personality. (Courtesy of Cline Library, Northern Arizona University.)

Georgie White and Harry Aleson took a bus from Boulder City, Nevada, to Peach Springs, Arizona. They stripped down to swimsuits, tennis shoes, and shirts and asked the sheriff to ship their clothes to Boulder City. Each wore a life preserver and backpack. They hiked 20 miles into the canyon and prepared to swim the Colorado River to Lake Mead. Years later, White operated a rafting business, shown here on the Colorado River. (Courtesy of Gene Segerblom.)

Georgie White and her Royal River Rats are shown at Temple Bar in July 1956. White was the first woman to run a commercial rafting business on the Colorado River. She used large, army surplus rubber rafts and often lashed them together for stability. White led her last trip at the age of 80. (Courtesy of National Park Service.)

Murl Emery's airplane engine–propelled flat boat, the *Flying Fish*, was used in photographic surveys of the Colorado River. Shown here is an excursion taken between the dam and Jumbo Wash in 1935.

This ferry landing on the Arizona side of the Colorado River near the mouth of Black Canyon was used as the Boulder Grand Canyon Navigation Company's terminal. Shown from left to right are Jayne Yowell Brubaker, Margaret Brubaker, Walter Brubaker, and five unidentified dam workers.

This view of the Colorado River is 30 miles downstream from the dam. Murl Emery's landing, at the mouth of the Eldorado Canyon, was the gathering spot of southern Nevada fishermen. The facilities included a café, trailer park, cabins, and boat dock. The National Park Service took control and renamed the area Nelson's Landing. It was closed after a 1974 flood destroyed the landing and took several lives.

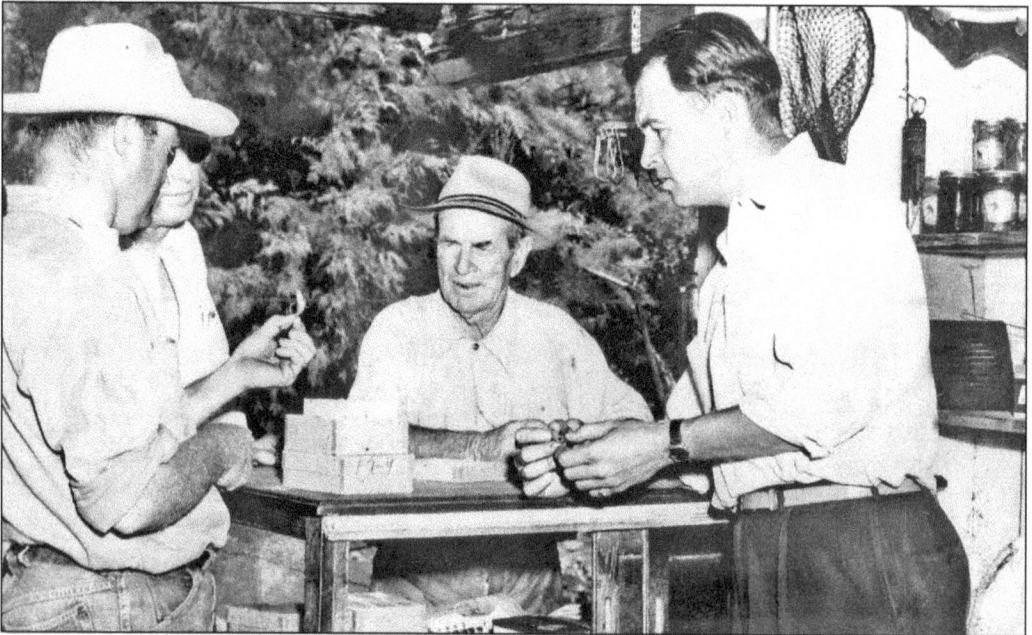

The trout fishermen shown are discussing fishing lures at Murl Emery's fishing dock. Charley Niehuis asked Emery how he happened to settle here and he replied, "My folks were taking us to California. We came to the old aerial ferry, which was called 'The Searchlight Ferry.' Dad had the money to pay for everyone's passage except mine, and I didn't have thirty-five cents either. . . . So I had to stay."

Leonard Atkinson (left) and Murl Emery are shown trout fishing near Emery's Landing. Emery had settled on the Colorado River long before the dam was built. He ferried the first engineers through Black Canyon to make the preliminary survey for the Boulder Canyon Project. The river in this area became a trout paradise after completion of the dam because the water was kept cooler than in other areas.

About 1923, the Bureau of Reclamation asked Murl Emery for help in checking out the sites proposed for the dam. Murl built an airboat using a World War I surplus airplane engine. The boat was designed in a way that it could be maneuvered over sandbars. Its maximum speed was estimated to be about 25 miles an hour. This is a view of the air-propelled boat used on the Colorado River below Boulder Dam. (Courtesy of Bureau of Reclamation.)

The Lake Mead National Recreation Area allows concessionaires to provide services in the recreation area. There are boat rentals at the marinas. A variety of cruises are offered on a paddle-wheel boat on Lake Mead. A guided trip may be taken by raft, canoe, or kayak. This image, taken just downstream of Hoover Dam, shows groups of people preparing to take a trip down the Colorado River. (Photograph by Andrew Pernick; courtesy of Bureau of Reclamation.)

Five

THE RESERVOIR

This photograph, taken by Laurence Klauber in April 1931, is a view of the Boulder Basin before the rise of Lake Mead. The Bureau of Reclamation gave responsibility for the area around the dam and reservoir to the National Park Service. At first, it was named Boulder Dam Lake and the Boulder Dam Recreation Area. The name of the lake was changed to Lake Mead in honor of Dr. Elwood Mead. In 1947, the National Park Service changed the name to Lake Mead National Recreation Area. In 1964, the Lake Mead National Recreation Area was officially designated as the first national recreation area after being called such since 1947. The Lake Mead National Recreation Area became a popular tourist destination. Miles of scenic beauty, fishing, hiking, mountain climbing, boating, swimming, and year-round sunshine appeal to a variety of interests.

This view looks across the reservoir area in 1932. It will be submerged when the dam is completed. The flat-topped hill in the center of the picture will form a small island. On February 1, 1935, a steel gate was lowered over the mouth of the last open diversion tunnel and the reservoir began to form.

The tourist stand here was a way to greet visitors and give information. It was difficult to miss the "Welcome Lake Mead" sign. Tourists could buy postcards, maps, and other souvenirs from the Boulder Dam Tourist Bureau. The stand was located near the mouth of Hemenway Wash. (Courtesy of National Park Service.)

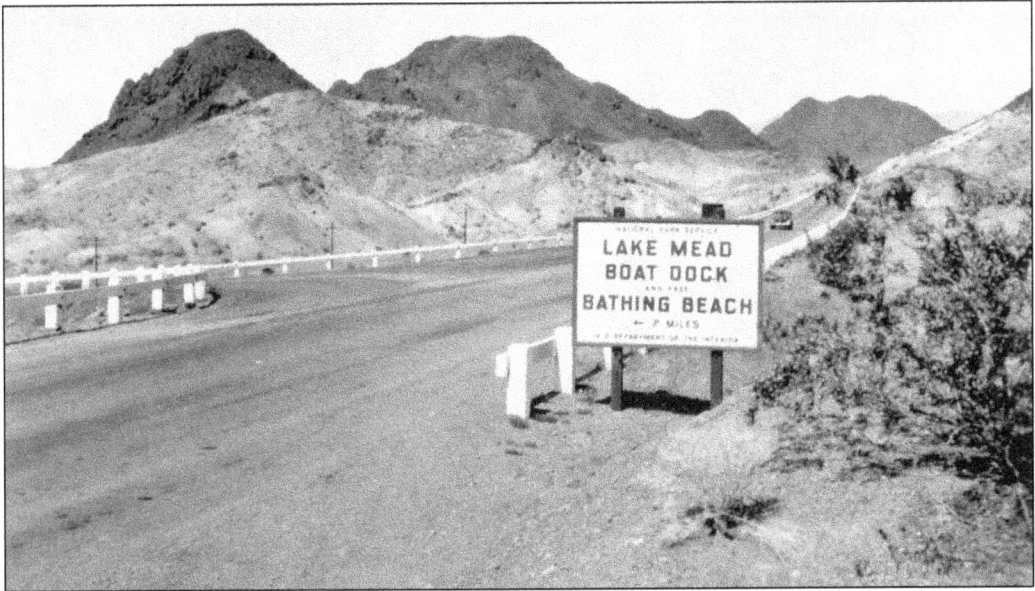

This sign shows the "short-cut" road to Lake Mead. The beach development by the National Park Service can be seen in this photograph. The Civilian Conservation Corps (CCC) helped the park service build the facilities. They cleared beaches for bathing and built tables, benches, and portable bathhouses. The CCC boys hauled a huge stockpile of sand so a 4,000-square-foot beach could be built. As the lake rose, they would have to rake the beach farther back. (Above courtesy of National Park Service; below courtesy of Bureau of Reclamation.)

A swim meet between the schoolchildren of Boulder City can be seen at the National Park Service bathing beach. Swimming lessons were offered to the children. (Courtesy of Bureau of Reclamation.)

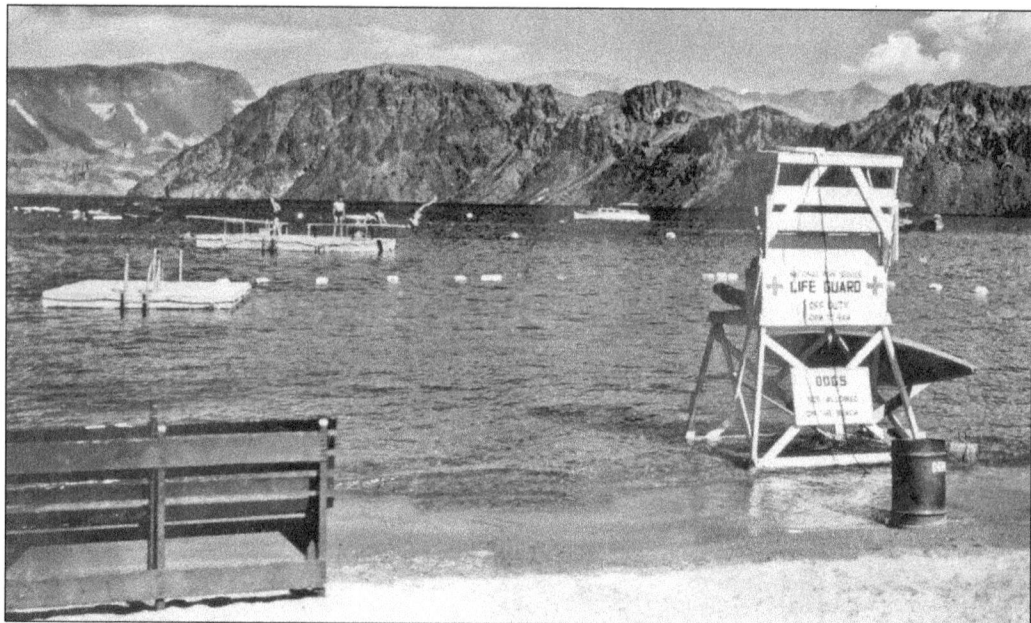

A bathing beach was constructed by the Civilian Conservation Corps (CCC) under the direction of the National Park Service. The beach, located in Hemenway Wash on the shore of Lake Mead, is pictured here on September 16, 1938.

Two Army Air Corps amphibian planes were flown to Nevada from Coronado, California, and test-landed on the rising lake. One of those planes is pictured here while taxiing to a mooring on the Boulder Canyon Reservoir on May 15, 1935.

This houseboat is shown on Lake Mead near the Boulder City boat landing. It was the first of its type to be launched on the lake. Today Lake Mead concessionaires offer houseboat rentals. It is a popular way to vacation on the lake. (Courtesy of National Park Service.)

In improving the recreation area in the 1950s, the park service added directional signs that were placed to mark each area of the park. This sign with the trademark jumping bass, marked LMNRA, was seen on entering the park from Boulder City. The National Park Service maintained the campground pictured here. Campers could pitch a tent. It was well developed with shade trees, running water, and modern restrooms. (Both courtesy of National Park Service.)

The campfire lecture, as viewed here, was a popular gathering at the small outdoor theater. Naturalists would tell of the wonders of the area. The talks were illustrated with color slides. Many of the visitors decided to stay longer when learning about the attractions in the area. (Both courtesy of National Park Service.)

The Lake Shore Trailer Court was on the shores of Lake Mead, five miles from Boulder City. The entrance is shown here. They advertised that there were 45 modern hook-ups for trailers with patios; some of the trailers are shown here. The amenities also included a grocery with fresh meats, beer, and soft drinks; a recreation room with television; tile showers; toilets; and a laundry. Later it became the Lake Shore Trailer Village. (Both courtesy of National Park Service.)

The Lake Mead National Recreation Area is administered from the Boulder City headquarters. One of the jobs to be done was to provide shady picnic spots, as seen here. Visitors could bring their own food and gear and use the free picnic area for an inexpensive meal. The CCC helped the park service by planting shade trees.

Many visitors to the Boulder Dam and the area camped in the new park service trailer camp, where life was easy and relaxed. Seen here, this camp overlooks Lake Mead and Fortification Mountain. The new camp had modern restrooms, water, electric outlets for trailers, and built-in electric stoves that could be rented for a small fee. (Courtesy of Bureau of Reclamation.)

The Grand Canyon–Boulder Dam Tours flyer above advertises tours for fishing and sightseeing and announces the opening of the new Hualapai Lodge. This aerial view is of the lodge with the lake in the background. The lodge was part of the expansion plan inaugurated by the Grand Canyon–Boulder Dam Tours. Glover Ruckstell's company entered into an agreement with the park service to provide all the recreational facilities. The lodge was built in 1941 and offered new tourist accommodations in the recreation area. The facility had three large buildings. The center building housed a curio shop, offices, assembly rooms, kitchen, dining room, employee quarters, and four bedrooms. In this 1945 image, the name had been changed to the Lake Mead Lodge to tie in better with the surroundings.

The Lake Mead Lodge, formerly Hualapai Lodge, is seen in 1945. The rooms were all air-conditioned by the most modern refrigerating equipment and had electric heat for the winter nights. The informal atmosphere of the desert oasis lodge provided quiet and comfort, but for entertainment and amusement, Las Vegas was only a short drive away. The buildings on either side of the center building contained 18 rooms, each with a private bath. Year-round fishing was possible, with boats and tackle available to rent.

Glover Ruckstell and Bill Messick are shown at the boat dock. In the early 1920s, Glover Ruckstell invented an axle for Model T trucks and became a millionaire. He had been involved in automobile racing, but his main interest was aviation. His company, Grand Canyon–Boulder Dam Tours (GCBDT), was the first enterprise to provide comprehensive tourist services. The company offered luxury hotel accommodations, boat tours, motor tours, and flights.

After the dam was finished, control of all lands of the federal project, except for the dam and Boulder City, was transferred from the Bureau of Reclamation to the National Park Service. Millionaire Glover Ruckstell wanted to secure an exclusive concession from the park service to build, own, and operate all tourist facilities within the recreation area. After much political negotiation, the concession was awarded. This view of the Lake Mead boat dock was taken around 1938. (Original work the property of the University of Nevada–Las Vegas, Las Vegas, Nevada.)

The development plan known as "Mission 66" was the result of the mid-1950s discussions between Nevada senator Alan Bible and park service officials. A view of the visitor center, just after completion around 1966, is shown here. The center, known as the Alan Bible Visitor Center, serves as an information center. Discovering the Desert, an interactive, hands-on exhibit, invites visitors to discover the Mohave Desert. Books and other educational and fun items are for sale, and the proceeds benefit the Lake Mead National Recreation Area. (Courtesy of National Park Service.)

At the time this aerial view of Boulder Beach was taken, Boulder City was no longer a federal reservation. The Bureau of Reclamation had quitclaimed all land, property, and infrastructure and had given the town 33 square miles of the surrounding desert. The National Park Service continued to administer the recreation area. The development of the beach, campground, trailer park, and lodge are seen in 1960. (Courtesy of National Park Service.)

Billed as the Lake Mead Sweepstakes Regatta, the national outboard championship races were run at Lake Mead near Boulder City October 25–27, 1946. This view of the packed parking area is an indication of the large crowd that attended this event. Members of the Boulder City Junior Chamber of Commerce (Jaycees), who sponsored the event, believed that this would become an annual event. Top-flight racers from all over the country took part in the regatta, which was made possible by the support of the businesses of Boulder City and Las Vegas. The Jaycees refreshment stand was a popular spot, as seen in the photograph below.

The Lake Mead Sweepstakes Regatta was sanctioned by the American Powerboat Association and conducted at Boulder Beach by the Associated Speedboat Clubs. Due to high winds, some of the events had to be postponed until the next month and run off at the Salton Sea Regatta in California. Shown is the parking area, the judges' stand, and starting clock.

Regarding fishing on Lake Mead, "If you take the time to get acquainted with the lake and its angling peculiarities, you'll have more than reasonable success," was the advice from Charley Niehuis in the March 1956 issue of *Arizona Highways*. The fishermen shown here are cruising on the clear waters of Lake Mead in 1939. (Courtesy of Bureau of Reclamation.)

The Izaak Walton League is an American association that was founded in 1922 to preserve fishing streams. Today the league is considered one of the oldest and most respected conservation organizations in the country. Walton's book the *Compleat Angler* was first published in 1653. Members of the Izaak Walton League are shown displaying a portion of a day's catch of Lake Mead bass on March 25, 1939. (Courtesy of Bureau of Reclamation.)

A 1940s scene of fishermen shows, from left to right, Collin Topley, John Howard, Fred MacMurray, and ? Cole. Cole was in charge of fishing activities at Lake Mead for the Grand Canyon–Boulder Dam Tours. It was reported the MacMurray caught two 5-pound bass. Fred MacMurray appeared in more than 100 films from the 1930s to the 1970s. He played the father, Steve Douglas, on the television show My Three Sons from 1961 to 1972. (Courtesy of Bureau of Reclamation.)

As a fisherman's paradise, Lake Mead had few rivals. In March 1939, when this photograph of fishermen casting alongside the Arizona intake towers was taken, the recreation area had already become a popular fishing destination. (Courtesy of Bureau of Reclamation.)

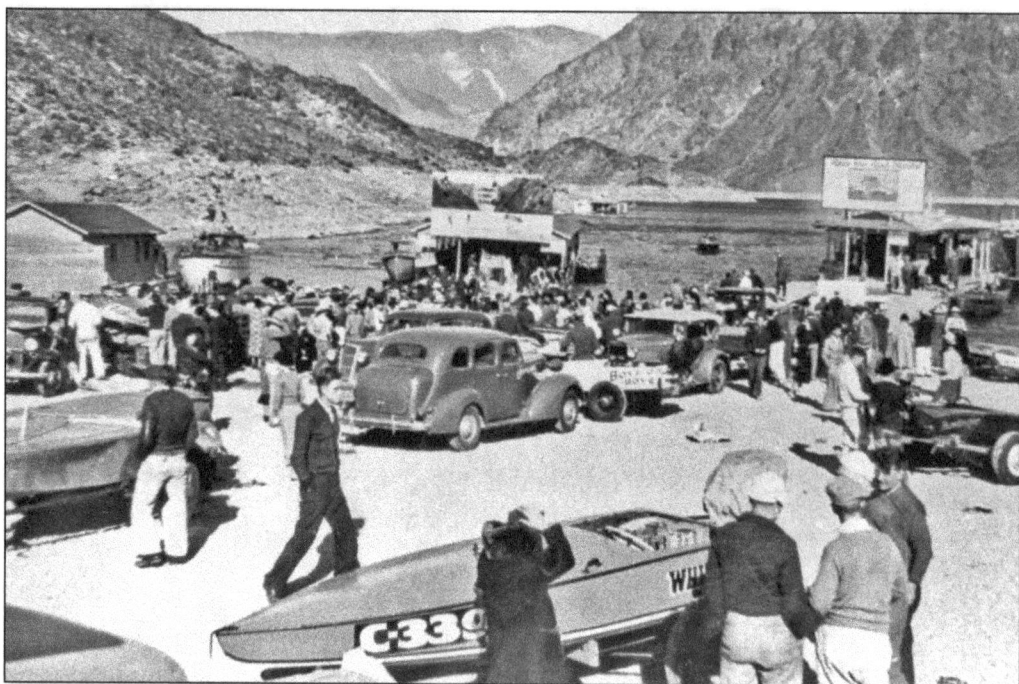

This view of the busy boat landing at Hemenway Wash shows Cashman's Scenic Cruises on the left and Murl Emery's "red boats." Cruisers would leave from these docks to make scheduled trips up the Colorado River. (Courtesy of Bureau of Reclamation.)

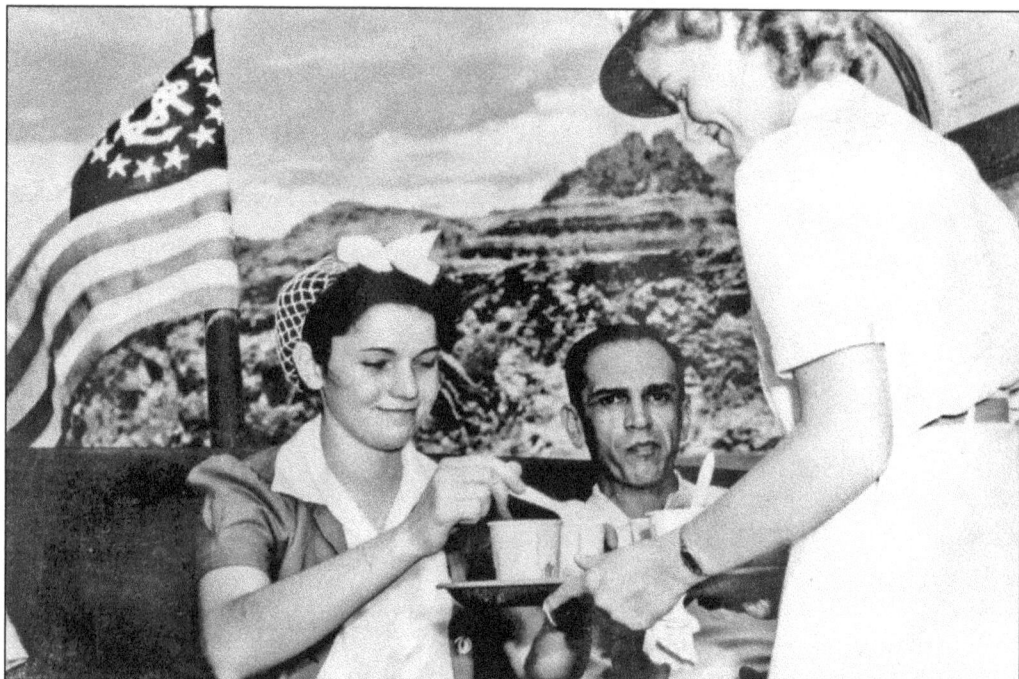

The "Scenic Lake Mead" cruises offered completely air-conditioned cabins so that even on the hottest summer day, the trip could be made. This tourist seems to be enjoying the service on this 1940 cruise. (Courtesy of Bureau of Reclamation.)

Jack Burrud, the "Sun Valley Bronco," established the official world's record for aquaplanes in endurance and distance on Lake Mead. Boulder Dam and intake towers are seen in the background. (Courtesy of Bureau of Reclamation.)

It is not unusual to see sailboats on Lake Mead. Newspaperman Elton Garrett once commented, "On Sunday the white sails far out on Lake Mead, put real tone into the sight of the blue water with its colorful rugged hills." In 1964, a small group of sailors formed the Nevada Sailing Club. A 45-foot sailboat sailing between Black and Boulder Canyons is seen in this photograph. (Courtesy of Bureau of Reclamation.)

This park service boat was named the *Lt. J. C. Ives*. In 1858, a small party of men led by Lt. J. C. Ives attempted to navigate the Colorado River upstream in the *Explorer*. After considerable difficulty, the boat emerged at the foot of Fortification Hill, where they turned back downstream. In his report to Congress, Ives said, "The Black Canyon is, of course, altogether worthless." Ives would be astounded to visit the area today. (Courtesy of National Park Service.)

Boulder Beach is shown on July 5, 1952. The holiday visitors are enjoying the bathing beach on the hot summer day. The bathing rafts were built by the Civilian Conservation Corps. (Courtesy of National Park Service.)

102

On February 6, 1936, Secretary of the Interior Harold Ickes announced that, in honor of the late Dr. Elwood Mead, the reservoir formed by the construction of Boulder Dam was officially named Lake Mead. Dr. Mead died on January 26, 1936. As commissioner of reclamation from 1924 to 1936, Dr. Mead supervised the building of Hoover Dam. Dr. Mead was an eminent engineer, a humane administrator, and beloved by all his associates. William Ekwall (left) and John C. Page, acting commissioner of reclamation, are seen at the September 29, 1936, dedication of a plaque honoring Dr. Mead. Page served as office engineer for the Boulder Canyon Project, in Boulder City, from 1930 to 1935. Dr. Mead said in advocating the development of the recreational features of the lake that he believed as many as 500,000 people annually would eventually visit it to see the magnificent vistas and to fish and bathe in its clear waters. In 2008, the park service announced that 8 million people a year visit Lake Mead National Recreation Area. (Courtesy of Bureau of Reclamation.)

The 1938 Neville expedition was a 650-mile journey from Green River, Wyoming, to Boulder Dam. The participants shown here are, from left to right, (first row) Bill Gibson, Dr. Elzada Clover, Lois Jotter, and Eugene Atkinson; (second row) Del Reed, Norman Neville, and Emery Kolb. The trip was made in light 15-foot boats. Kolb and his brother Ellsworth were the first to record the trip through the Grand Canyon on motion-picture film. (Courtesy of National Park Service.)

Glover Ruckstell built the boat landing on Lake Mead, shown here, for his Grand Canyon–Boulder Dam Tours. GCBDT offered plane trips to the Grand Canyon and cruises to Boulder Dam and the Grand Canyon. (Courtesy of Bureau of Reclamation.)

Buzz Holmstrom is shown greeting Lois Jotter and Dr. Elzada Clover in August 1938. Dr. Clover, 41-year-old University of Michigan botany instructor, and her assistant, Lois Jotter, descended the Green River to the Colorado River, then on to Boulder Dam. The women were the first women to brave the rapids of the Colorado River in a descent by boat. Dr. Clover returned to Boulder City in 1945 to study the manner in which plant life in the Grand Canyon and Lake Mead were affected by the formation of the reservoir. (Courtesy of National Park Service.)

Gorgeous scenery awaits these tourists as they cruise into the lower end of the Grand Canyon. During high water, it was possible to travel up the canyon as far as Quartermaster by cruiser. Small boats, available for charter work at Pierce Ferry, could go even farther. (Courtesy of Bureau of Reclamation.)

Murl Emery developed a cruise line of red boats. He publicized the line with "Ride the Red Boats." Glover Ruckstell made an agreement with both Emery and Jim Cashman to provide cruise service. The Red Line dock can be seen in this photograph of a park service barge being launched at the boat landing. (Courtesy of National Park Service.)

Jim Cashman arrived in the tent town of Las Vegas in 1904. One of the jobs "Big Jim" found was repairing telephone lines around Searchlight (a bigger town than Las Vegas). He got a contract to haul ore from the mines. To reach the railroad in Kingman, he set up his own ferry to cross the Colorado River. He opened the Searchlight Garage and an automobile dealership. Cashman's boat docks are seen here. (Courtesy of Bureau of Reclamation.)

With the dam behind them, these two boats speed through the calm waters of Lake Mead and stir up a foaming wake. Water sports enthusiasts find Lake Mead a perfect place to enjoy their pursuits. The National Park Service, with help from the Civilian Conservation Corps, removed driftwood from 200 miles of lakeshore to make boating safe. (Courtesy of Bureau of Reclamation.)

Spectacular scenery can be found around Lake Mead. After an active day on the lake, this evening view provides a calming and relaxing atmosphere. (Courtesy of Bureau of Reclamation.)

Six

THE BOULDER DAM HOTEL

In the spring of 1933, Paul "Jim" Webb applied for a permit to build an elegant hotel in Boulder City; the Bureau of Reclamation granted the permit. The Boulder Dam Hotel opening was a gala event on December 15 and 16, 1933. The hotel was the only luxury hotel in southern Nevada, and many famous guests stayed there. Howard Hughes, who had crashed an airplane in Lake Mead, stayed at the hotel to recuperate. This 1939 view of the hotel shows the Uptown Hardware store and apartments under construction in the background. (Original work the property of the University of Nevada–Las Vegas, Las Vegas, Nevada.)

Views of the interior of the lobby and guest room of the recently completed Boulder Dam Hotel are seen here. The hotel operated under government permit. The lobby was paneled in southern gumwood, and the chandeliers and wall sconces gave off a soft glow. Guests enjoyed sitting in the cozy lobby, especially around the fireplace, on a cold winter's night. The guest rooms were light and airy. It was said that the hotel compares in beauty with famous hotels but has the advantage of smallness. The lobby today has the same paneling and lighting. In 1982, the National Trust for Historic Preservation listed the hotel on the National Register of Historic Places. The Boulder Dam Hotel is owned and operated by the nonprofit Boulder City Museum and Historical Association. The hotel has 20 guest rooms, unique shops, an art gallery, the Boulder City/Hoover Dam Museum, a restaurant, facilities for small conferences, and a research facility.

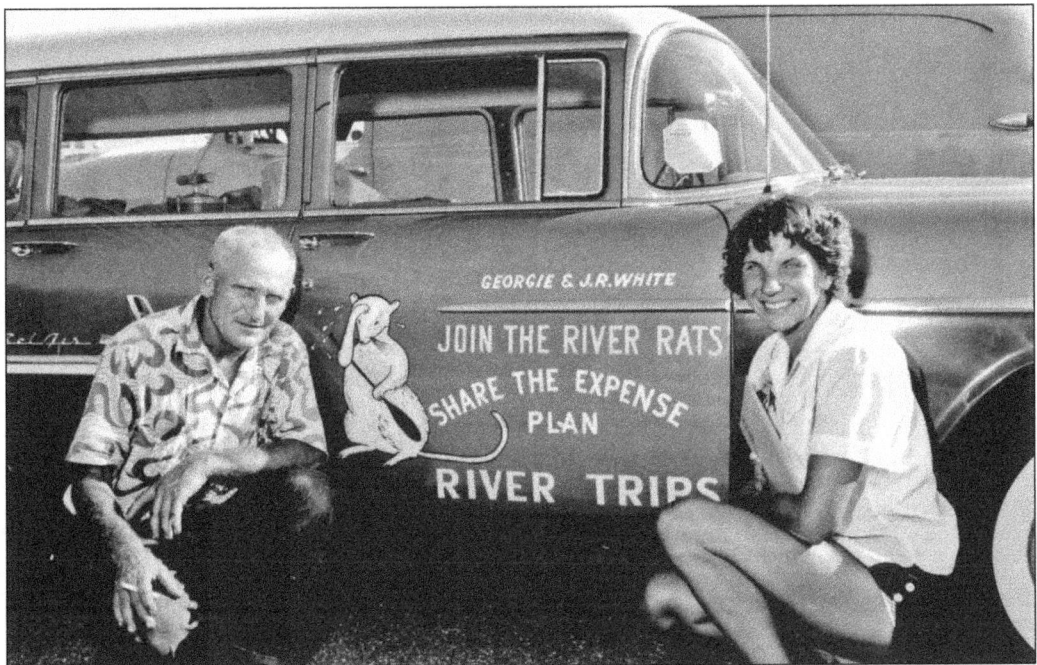

In 1960, Hal Brown took charge of the hotel. He put pink and green neon lights up and down the Colonial pillars and along the eaves. He paved the terrace and turned the fountain into a barbecue pit. In the lobby, he installed a newsstand and pop cooler and put a television in the fireplace; the chamber of commerce used a corner for an office. River runner Georgie White used the hotel as a base for her Colorado River trips. Travelers met at the hotel, were picked up by bus, and after a few weeks would return. White and J. R. Clark are shown above, in Boulder City, with their new car. The River Rats meet in the lobby below; White is in the center with knee bent. (Above courtesy of Cline Library, Northern Arizona University.)

American composer Ferde Grofe lived at the hotel off and on for almost a year. He came to the hotel to establish residence for a divorce. The proceedings took much longer than expected. Grofe was in love with musician Anne Lampton. The Las Vegas wedding of Lampton and Grofe is pictured here. Grofe was the composer of the *Grand Canyon Suite*. Grofe's room was on the second-floor corner of the southeast wing, where he composed music. Grofe, shown at the Lake Mead Observation Point, was inspired to write *Dawn over Lake Mead* while he and Anne were watching the sun rise over Lake Mead.

Shirley Temple went to school for the first time in Boulder City. The nine-year-old and her parents arrived at the hotel on May 30, 1938. Following dinner, they took a special tour of the dam. The next day, Temple visited all the grades and posed for photographs in front of the hotel and the school. Temple said, "Mother, I think school is swell." This photograph is from the 1930s.

Will Rogers, shown here, a friend of Glover Ruckstell, stayed at the hotel for a few weeks. Each night, the popular entertainer performed to a packed house at the Boulder Theatre. A story is told that Rogers and Supt. Frank Crowe were having lunch in the Anderson Mess Hall. Rogers asked Crowe how many men he had working. Crowe answered, "About half of them." Rogers replied "Mr. Crowe, I'm supposed to be the comedian." Several months later, Will Rogers was killed in a plane crash.

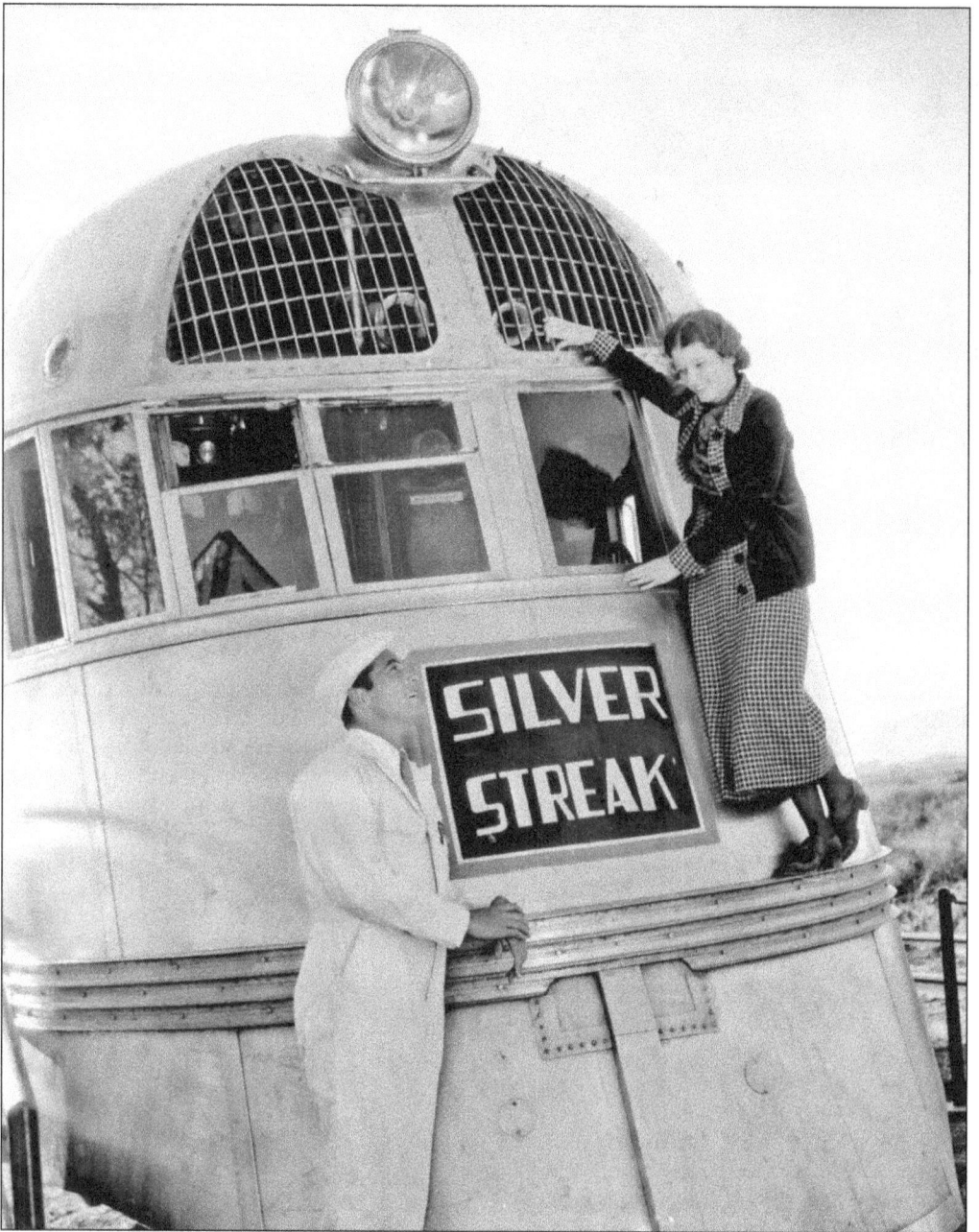

Jean Page, daughter of Boulder Canyon Project office engineer John Page, is seen with a star of the film *The Silver Streak*, Charles Starrett. A record-breaking run made the Zephyr train so famous its next trip was to Hollywood. RKO Pictures produced this 1934 movie. Some scenes from the motion picture were filmed at Boulder Dam. The cast and crew stayed at the Boulder Dam Hotel, and the world premiere was held at the Boulder Theatre. Jean Page recalled that Walker Young, the construction engineer of the project, was out of town. Young usually saw to influential guests, so her father was in charge. Jean had the opportunity to meet the cast and crew. She even went to Hollywood and was given the part of a nurse. Several local residents were given a chance to appear in the motion picture.

The actors from the RKO Pictures film *The Silver Streak* are shown filming on location at Boulder Dam. The film is an adventure tale about the railroad industry and a young designer who is responsible for a super-fast train. The train has the critical task of transporting an iron lung across the country to save the son of a railroad president from polio. This publicity still from *The Silver Streak* shows the actors.

BOULDER CITY HOOVER DAM MUSEUM

Construction of Hoover Dam & Boulder City as told by the workers and their families.

**Located in the Historic
Boulder Dam Hotel
In the heart of Boulder City
1305 Arizona Street
702-294-1988
bcmha@yahoo.com**

Interest in building a museum began about the same time construction of the dam began. The Boulder City Museum and Historical Association was incorporated in 1981. Over the next several years, the association considered several locations for a museum. The museum opened in 1988 when a local couple, Liz and Kae Pohe, offered space in their store. In 1993, it was rumored that the historic Boulder Dam Hotel would be torn down. A group of Boulder City residents formed an association to save the hotel. The Boulder City Museum and Historical Association, chamber of commerce, arts council, and the city formed the Boulder Dam Hotel Association. The hotel association and the community worked together to raise funds to do an adaptive reuse of the building. The plan included moving the museum into the hotel, which it did in 1998 while the renovation continued. In 2001, the last phase, the hotel rooms, was finished. Four years later, the members of the hotel association agreed that the Boulder City Museum and Historical Association should take over sole responsibility for the hotel. On September 5, 2005, it became official. This museum brochure pictures some highlights of the museum, which is about the people who built Hoover Dam.

Seven

ON THE OUTSKIRTS
OF TOWN

This 1931 aerial view of Boulder Dam shows the location of Boulder City (upper edge near center). Boulder City was a federal reservation until 1960. The government did not allow gambling or alcohol. The citizens of Boulder City did not approve alcohol until 1970 and still have not approved gaming. Boulder City is the only town in Nevada that outlaws gambling. The Railroad Pass area had been a mining district since the early 1900s and was outside the reservation. In 1931, a gaming license was issued and the Railroad Pass Club was opened. At the other end of town, there was a mining claim within the land that government had withdrawn for the Boulder Canyon Project. In the 1950s, some businessmen became aware of the mining claim, bought it, and opened the Gold Strike Inn. Today both properties have added hotels and are still open for business, although the Gold Strike is now named the Hacienda. (Courtesy of Bureau of Reclamation.)

Shown laying out the Gold Strike Hotel building around 1956 are, from left to right, Don Belding, owner; O. L. Raney, owner; Glen Stark, contractor; and Jack Richardson, owner. The business partners found out there was some land on the way to the dam that was an ancient mining claim. Though there were heirs somewhere, they had not bothered to look at their inheritance. After some detective work and a visit from an out-of-state lawyer, the land deal was closed. To quote the lawyer when asked what the asking price would be, he looked at the rocky mountain terrain and said, "If it were mine I would give it to you."

This popular southern Nevada stop is the Gold Strike Inn. This image shows the inn after opening in May 1958. Located on Highway 93, three miles from the dam, the Gold Strike was a favorite of the boating crowd. It offered six slot machines, a gift shop, snack bar, cocktail lounge, and service station. The Gold Strike had a unique entrance that displayed an old miner and burro pulling an ore car.

This is a view of the Gold Strike and the items from the "Dobie Doc" Caudill collection of artifacts of Nevada's past that has been moved from the Last Frontier Village in Las Vegas. The Gold Strike sat on a 120-acre parcel of land patented by building contractor Patrick J. Sullivan. Sullivan arrived in Las Vegas in 1906. He didn't build on the land but did some mining for gold and turquoise. The land was known as Sullivan's Gulch. The federal government withdrew land in the area but overlooked this piece, which has become an "island" in the middle of federal property. (Courtesy of National Park Service.)

For a time, the Gold Strike was known as Fort Lucinda. There was a narrow-gauge railroad that gave a view of Lake Mead during a 10-minute, one-mile ride around the mountain. In October 1966, Fort Lucinda closed its doors and sold the ghost town relics. It was reported that the train was removed to Elitch's Amusement Park in Denver, Colorado. (Courtesy of National Park Service.)

In the early 1900s, government survey teams looked at the gap between the mountain ranges that separate the Las Vegas Valley from the Eldorado Valley. They concluded that it was an ideal location for a railroad linking the mining town of Searchlight and Las Vegas. The gap was officially named Railroad Pass. In 1930, the Union Pacific Railroad built a branch from Las Vegas to Boulder City and the railroad tracks confirmed the name. In 1908, Camp Alunite was a thriving town at Railroad Pass. Many structures had been built, including an assay house equipped with a complete outfit. There were plans to build more. In the 1930s, there were two settlements: Texas Acres and Dee's Camp. In this 1949 aerial view of the Railroad Pass area, the casino can be seen below, left of center. The highway that connects Boulder City with Las Vegas runs in front of the buildings, and the railroad tracks run behind the building. The area known as Alunite is shown above center and across the highway. The dark spots above Alunite are Art Klinger's surplus ventilators.

Art Klinger can be seen among his surplus ventilators. To those who passed by, the 80 acres of rust-coated piles of iron and steel were considered a pile of junk. They would have been surprised that buyers from all over the country arrived at Klinger's door to buy his "junk."

The government had leftover ventilators, shown here, from the building of the Henderson, Nevada, Basic Magnesium plant. Art Klinger bought them. At the time of this photograph, Klinger had already sold enough of them to pay for the cost. Mace's Circle Bar and the Star Club can be seen in the distance.

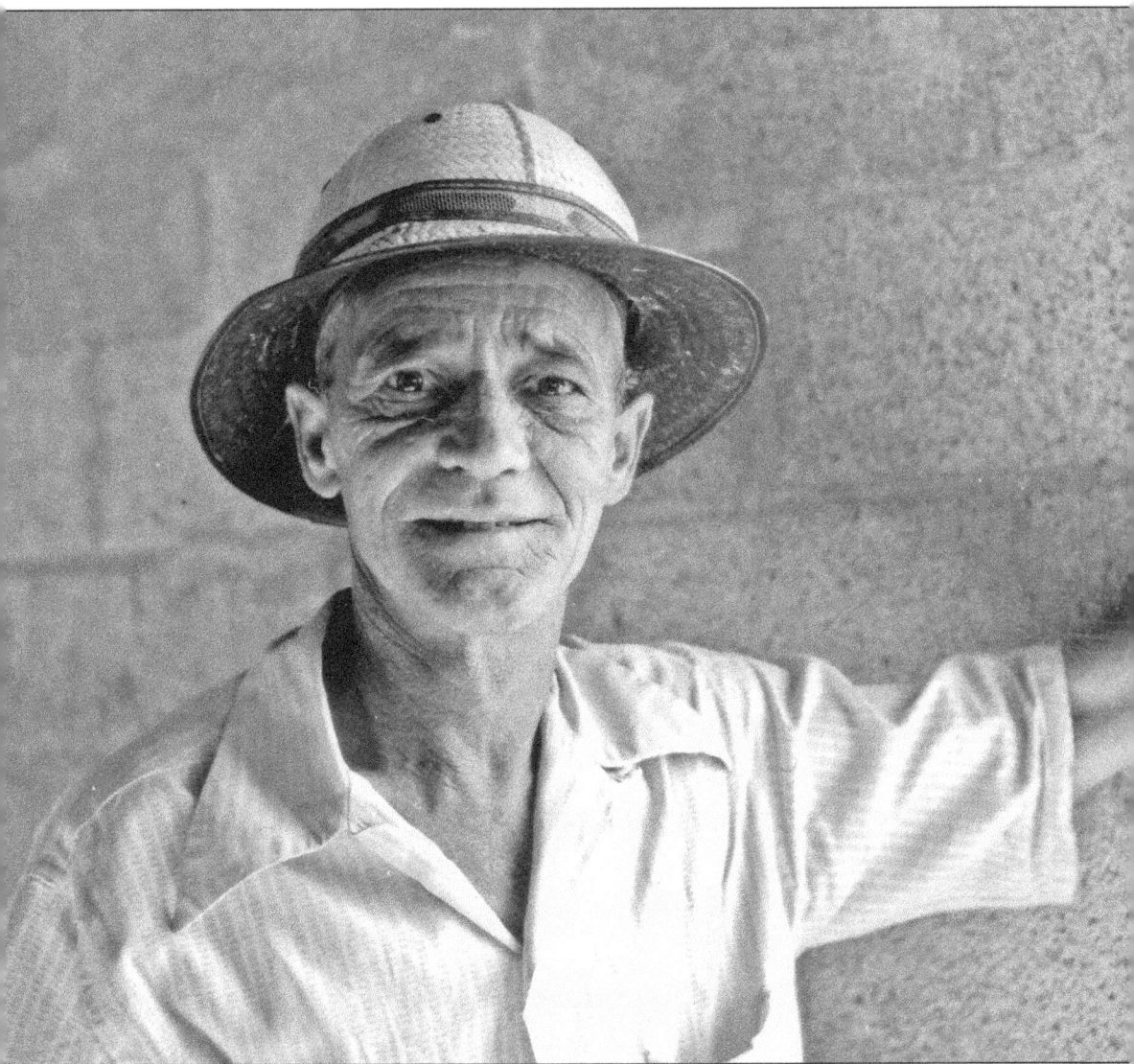

Arthur Klinger (pictured here in 1953) came to southern Nevada in 1932 with his wife, Sarah, and two eldest daughters, Doris and Betty. He worked as a machinist for the Six Companies, the builders of Hoover Dam. Housing for the family was difficult, so the family moved into a service station on land leased from the Bureau of Reclamation. The station burned, and the owner refused to rebuild, so Klinger obtained the lease and built another station with living quarters for his family. Many of the mine operators came to him for machine work, so he installed a machine shop; his business grew so much that he quit his job at Six Companies and worked full-time at his business. When the dam was finished, Klinger bought leftover steel equipment. Klinger was a World War I veteran and was active in Boulder City civic and political activities. He served as a director of the chamber of commerce, an active Rotarian, and a member of the Elks Lodge. His "junkyard" was actually a gold mine. Art Klinger was sometimes referred to as the Mayor of Railroad Pass.

The Railroad Pass area is seen in the early 1930s. The Boulder City branch line of the Union Pacific Railroad ran through here. Texas Acres and Dee's Camp were home to squatters and settlers as early as 1909. The Alunite Mining District is still listed on some maps of the area.

A gaming license was issued to F. J. Warren in 1931. The Bureau of Reclamation had declared their intention of keeping Boulder City free of gambling and liquor, but this area was just outside the reservation. A casino was built on O. D. Johnson's patent claim. The Railroad Pass Club opened its doors to the public on August 1, 1931. This Hobert Blair photograph is a view of the club at the time of the opening.

The Railroad Pass Club welcomed the workers and their families. The casino was cooled by 25 ceiling fans and many windows. This view of the bar and gaming pit is an indication that everyone enjoyed evenings of food, gambling, and dancing at Railroad Pass.

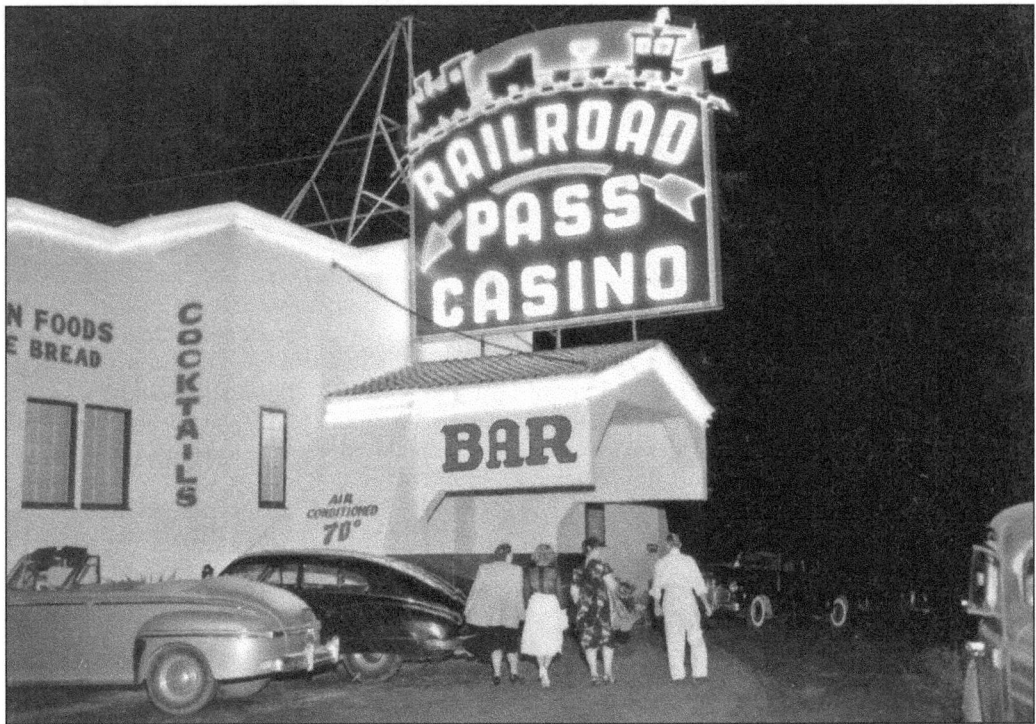

The Railroad Pass Casino holds the oldest active gaming license in southern Nevada. This 1948 view shows the neon sign and a family entering, possibly to celebrate an important event. It was advertised that the casino was an air-conditioned 70 degrees, an attraction in the desert heat. (Courtesy of Nevada State Museum–Las Vegas.)

To mark the 75th birthday of Boulder City, a laser light show was projected on the face of Hoover Dam. Shown is the logo created for the event. Invited guests met at the Boulder Dam Hotel and were taken by double-decker bus to the visitor center. Lee Tilman was invited to throw the switch for the ceremony. He arrived in the summer of 1931 and went to work on the Boulder Canyon Project. Tilman, the last known "31er," passed away on December 15, 2007, at the age of 94. His oral history is on file at the Boulder City Library and UNLV Special Collections. (Photograph by Jeremy Moore; courtesy of Bureau of Reclamation.)

BIBLIOGRAPHY

Allen, Marion. *Hoover Dam and Boulder City*. Redding, CA: CP Printing and Publishing, 1983.

Andress, Donna. *Eldorado Canyon and Nelson, Nevada, Historical Documents Reminiscences Commentary*. Essex, CA: Mojave Desert Heritage and Cultural Association, 1997.

Belknap, Buzz. *Belknap's Waterproof Grand Canyon River Guide, All New Edition*. Evergreen, CO: Westwater Books, 2007.

Dimock, Brad. *Every Rapid Speaks Plainly: The Salmon, Green, and Colorado River Journals of Buzz Holmstrom*. Flagstaff, AZ: Fretwater Press, 2003.

Dunar, Andrew, and Dennis McBride. *Building Hoover Dam: The Oral History of the Great Depression*. Reno, NV: University of Nevada Press, 1993.

Hansen, Oskar J. W. *Sculptures at Hoover Dam*. Washington, D.C.: Department of the Interior, U.S. Government Printing Office, 1968.

Kolvet, Renee Corona, and Victoria Ford. *The Civilian Conservation Corps in Nevada*. Reno, NV: University of Nevada Press, 2006.

McBride, Dennis. *Hard Work and Far From Home: The Civilian Conservation Corps at Lake Mead, NV*. Boulder City, NV: Boulder Images, 1995.

———. *In The Beginning, A History of Boulder City, NV*. Boulder City, NV: Boulder City/Hoover Dam Museum, 1992.

———. *Midnight on Arizona Street: The Secret Life of the Boulder Dam Hotel*. Boulder City, NV: Boulder City/Hoover Dam Museum, 1993.

Rhinehart, Julian. "The Grand Dam." *Nevada Magazine*, October 1995.

Stevens, Joseph. *Hoover Dam: An American Adventure*. Norman, OK: University of Oklahoma Press, 1988.

Vilander, Barbara. *Hoover Dam, The Photographs of Ben Glaha*. Tucson, AZ: University of Arizona Press, 1999.

Welch, Vince, Cort Conley, and Brad Dimock. *The Doing of the Thing: The Brief Brilliant Whitewater Career of Buzz Holmstrom*. Flagstaff, AZ: Fretwater Press, 2004.

Westwood, Richard E. *Woman of the River: Georgie White Clark, White-Water Pioneer*. Logan, UT: Utah State University Press, 1997.

Across America, People are Discovering Something Wonderful. *Their Heritage.*

Arcadia Publishing is the leading local history publisher in the United States. With more than 4,000 titles in print and hundreds of new titles released every year, Arcadia has extensive specialized experience chronicling the history of communities and celebrating America's hidden stories, bringing to life the people, places, and events from the past. To discover the history of other communities across the nation, please visit:

www.arcadiapublishing.com

Customized search tools allow you to find regional history books about the town where you grew up, the cities where your friends and family live, the town where your parents met, or even that retirement spot you've been dreaming about.

www.ingramcontent.com/pod-product-compliance
Lightning Source LLC
Chambersburg PA
CBHW080550110426

42813CB00006B/1270